MURDER &
MAYHEM
CANADIAN
GHOST STORIES

Dawn Sutherland

QUAGMIRE PRESS

© 2015 by Quagmire Press Ltd.
First printed in 2015   10 9 8 7 6 5 4 3 2 1
Printed in Canada

The Publisher: Quagmire Press Ltd.
Website: www.quagmirepress.com

Library and Archives Canada Cataloguing in Publication
Sutherland, Dawn, 1962-, author
    Murder and mayhem Canadian ghost stories / Dawn Sutherland.

ISBN 978-1-926695-24-2 (paperback).— ISBN 978-1-926695-26-6 (pdf)

    1. Murder. 2. Haunted places. I. Title.

HV6515.S87 2016   364.152'3   C2016-903664-2

Project Director: Hank Boer
Editor: Wendy Pirk
Cover Image: dark house © MoreenBlackthorne / Thinkstock ; aurora
© Neutronman / Thinkstock; Abstract vector shiny background © -strizh-
/ Thinkstock; Foggy path in the woods © srbphotography1 / Thinkstock;
Aurora Borealis © Prasit Rodphan / Thinkstock

Produced with the assistance of the Government of
Alberta, Alberta Media Fund.

Alberta
Government

PC: 32

DEDICATION

For Garry, with love.

Acknowledgements

~

Thank you seems so inadequate to show the kind of appreciation an author feels when the words they put together evolve into the finished product you now have in your hand. Life is really a team sport, and I am ever so grateful for each member of the talented staff at Quagmire Press.

Thank you to Hank Boer, the captain of our flotilla, for your foresight, ideas and guidance.

Thank you to Wendy Pirk, my wonderful editor who helped fine-tune these mysterious tales. Your sharp eye and attention to detail turned my many ramblings into a readable collection.

It never ceases to amaze me how stories morph over the years and through many retellings. I've made my best effort to blend the varied details from as many credible sources and variations of each tale as possible, and a huge thank you must be expressed to the original chroniclers, many talented researchers, writers, journalists, bloggers and record keepers who came before and laid the foundation for these stories.

And finally, thank you to my long-suffering family. As I've said many, many times over, without you all this, or anything else I do, would be meaningless.

Contents

Introduction

~

Chances are we all know what it's like to have a troubled spirit. We wouldn't be human if we didn't wrestle with relationships or finances or jobs, or any number of life's issues. All of these situations can leave us in a state of turmoil as we struggle to find the best way to handle them. And the more important or complicated an issue is, the bigger the inner struggle we face.

Sometimes this internal tug-of-war follows us when we leave our earthly lives, inhibiting our ability to pass on to a restful afterlife. And so it is that the spirit or soul of a deceased individual continues to wander this earth, often attempting to remain in the place where it once lived and either try to contact the people it once knew, or haunt any newcomer who takes up residence. Perhaps the spirit longs to make amends for some perceived hurt or remain connected to a loved one; sometimes the desire to complete an unfinished task is what keeps it from moving on. Whatever ties it to the physical world, the spirit persists in an effort to attain some measure of peace and, ultimately, set itself free.

To prepare for this collection, I read through seemingly endless documents discussing ghosts and the many theories about why they exist. Does someone become a ghost by choice or by chance? Are some people just doomed to spend eternity aimlessly meandering the physical world and never obtaining that peaceful afterlife we all desire? Or is it circumstance that inhibits the soul's smooth transition into the spirit world? Admittedly the situation is different in many a supernatural tale, but not so for the ghosts in this collection. The spirits seen or experienced in these stories became stuck in space and time, unable to move on from this world because they met a violent end.

In some of the following tales, the troubled spectres are doomed to roam this earth because their lives were brutally cut short by the actions of another, and they are looking for justice. In other narratives, the spirit can't rest because the person was put to death as a consequence of a murder he or she committed. In all cases, the spirits in this collection have been unleashed because of some type of brutality. They are either sad or angry, and arguably more persistent and frightening than other apparitions might be.

Many would argue that it's impossible to write a true crime book about ghosts. When the project was first presented to me, I questioned the idea myself. After all, you can't get a more subjective topic to write about. How can you "prove" anything about a ghostly encounter, especially given the fact that several accounts seemingly based on the same spirit can vary drastically? One might also point out that seeing a ghost or experiencing supernatural phenomena tends to get one's emotions boiling over, and as we all know, details derived from an emotional testimony are typically unreliable.

With that in mind, in an effort to remain true to the non-fiction nature of this book and present as in-depth a story as possible, I tried not to rely solely on eyewitness accounts. So although the seeds for the stories in this volume frequently came from individual experiences, with few exceptions I've been able to track down newspaper articles or even trial transcripts describing the murder believed to be the impetus behind a ghost's origin. Also, each story has been published in several platforms over the years; and as we all know, stories that get told and retold have a way of undergoing a metamorphosis of sorts, so that details in one telling might not be the same as details in the next. For the stories in this book, I've made every effort to include as many varying details as possible while trying to maintain some kind of cohesive retelling.

It is my hope that you, the reader, whether you are a ghost story aficionado or someone who dedicates a great deal of effort to studying the paranormal, will find some measure of enjoyment in these pages.

Chapter 1

Daddy's Girl

~

Life in the early days of Canada's colonial history was an arduous existence with one struggle after another to overcome. Rare was the settler whose family was not touched by some form of tragedy. And many a time those tragedies were purposeful acts of violence that permanently changed people's lives, all in the name of greed.

In 1802, James King was one of many fur traders working with the North West Company. Major competition at the time came in the form of trappers working with the Hudson Bay Company and the XY Company. The official name of the XY Company was the New North West Company, but to avoid confusion with its North West Company rival, it distinguished its merchandise with the markings XY. King had been sent out to purchase furs from a group of Native hunters, something he'd done many times before. With three companies fighting for dominance, this type of mission was always a dangerous one. However, King's newest assignment was laced with even more danger than usual. His superiors had warned him of a ruthless man named La Mothe who worked for the XY Company and was after the very same furs King had been charged with obtaining. La Mothe would stop at nothing to get those furs.

King, a tough and rugged man in his own right, wasn't overly worried about his competition. He had come up against many a callous fur trader during his career, and he was confident he could handle himself against the worst of them. Besides, being forewarned is being forearmed; La Mothe wouldn't have the element of surprise on his side.

Setting out from his Fort Augustus home, which is now Fort Saskatchewan, Alberta, King kissed his wife and six-year-old daughter goodbye and promised he would return in three days. King's daughter was never happy when her daddy left home, but this time she was particularly edgy.

"Please don't go," King's daughter pleaded as he scooped her in his arms for a last hug and then handed her over to her mother.

"Don't you worry none," King chided. "Be a good girl and I'll be back before you know it."

King's wife was able to soothe their daughter the first day King was away, but by day two the little girl was beyond consoling. That night she woke screaming in the middle of the night. No amount of soothing and reassurance from mom could ease the child's fear. Over and over again she kept saying that she'd seen her father standing beside her bed. She knew it was him; she knew her daddy's eyes. But there was something wrong. He didn't smile, and his neck was all red. Usually, her dad would have smiled at her. He would have reached out for her, she was sure. Instead, he looked sad and far away, as if he was saying he was sorry for something.

The girl was out of sorts the next day, and that night she woke again and began sobbing hysterically. Once again she told her mother that she'd seen her daddy standing at the foot of her bed. Once again the little girl told about her daddy's sad eyes and red throat. The story mirrored the one from the night before almost word for word. King's wife tried to hide her own anxiety as she cuddled the little girl, stroking her hair and promising her everything would be just fine. King's wife was anxious for her husband's return so their daughter could regain some measure of peace. Truth be told, King's wife was also beginning to worry about her husband. Their daughter had never suffered from strange night terrors before, and the woman was beginning to fear that they might be an omen.

When King didn't return home when expected, his wife tried to ease her growing concern by reasoning that the poor weather might be to blame. When that excuse wore thin, even to her own ears, she began sharing her little girl's experiences with others at the fort. It was a bad dream spurred on by a little separation anxiety, her neighbours suggested. King's wife agreed—until King's bloody body was pulled into the fort. Despite being armed with the knowledge that La Mothe might challenge him for the coveted furs, King became embroiled in a bitter battle with La Mothe. King was shot through the neck on the same night that his daughter first woke up in tears.

The discovery of King's body left no doubt to anyone who heard the story that the man's spirit visited his daughter on the night of his demise. The father who loved his little girl more than life itself had reached out, not once, but twice, to say he was sorry and bid her one last farewell.

Chapter 2

Friends in this Life
and the Next

~

Sometimes you just know a true friend when you meet
one. Wellington Delaney Moses was that kind
of friend.

A barber by trade, Moses was among the first wave of
black settlers to flee slavery and migrate to Victoria, B.C. In
1858, Moses set up his first barbershop. As his business grew
and prospered, Moses gained the respect of his community. But
despite his obvious success, he couldn't shake the draw of adventure. The discovery of gold in BC's Cariboo Mountains in 1860
led to a migration of miners from as far away as California.
Moses knew his particular skill would be of some value to a
growing population of miners so he pulled up stakes once again,
leaving his business and his wife in Victoria.

Charles Morgan Blessing was one of many American
miners who wanted to try their hand at finding the mother lode.
He headed for the promised gold fields of Quesnel, Barkerville

and the Cariboo region in 1866, just a few years after Bill Barker discovered the precious metal along Williams Creek in 1862. Around the same time, Moses decided to venture further inland, and the two men met while travelling. Blessing was unlike other gold seekers in that he appeared quite well-to-do and was more interested in adventure than he was in striking it rich. The fact that Blessing wasn't singularly focused on staking a claim made him more approachable than most, and he and Moses forged an immediate bond. Theirs was the kind of friendship that could be a lifesaver when one was trekking through the wilderness at such a potentially volatile time; they had each other's backs.

The two men continued together on their journey until they met a fellow named James Barry. Unlike the immediate trust that had formed between Moses and Blessing, Moses took an instant dislike to Barry; he couldn't explain why, he just didn't trust him. Perhaps that was the reason Moses broke off from the group, deciding to stay an extra night when the three men arrived in Quesnel. The small community was in obvious need of a barber, and Moses knew he could make some quick cash before continuing on to Barkerville. Unhappy with Moses' change of plans but anxious to get to his destination, Blessing left his friend in Quesnel and continued on with Barry, but not before he and Moses agreed to reconnect a few days later at a predetermined location. Blessing was concerned for his personal safety. In particular, he told Moses he had a bad feeling about travelling with Barry. According to archival documents, Blessing left his friend with a final thought: "My name is Charles Morgan Blessing, be sure to recollect it if anything should happen to me in this country."

Moses wasn't far behind his former travel companions, arriving in Barkerville just a few days later. He immediately set up his barbershop along the community's main drag, and in no time at all people were lining up for a shave and a haircut. Although he was busy at his shop, Moses made good on his promise to meet with Blessing at the previously agreed upon meeting place. The problem was, although Moses made it on time, Blessing was nowhere to be seen. Furthermore, when Moses asked after the man, no one remembered seeing anyone of Blessing's description. Moses knew any number of situations could have delayed his friend, and Moses was confident that sooner or later Blessing would make it to the barbershop; most of the miners in the area eventually did. But as time passed and Blessing had yet to make an appearance, the barber felt a growing sense of concern.

Then one day James Barry turned up, needing a barber. Had Barry been aware that the establishment belonged to his former travelling companion, he may have chosen to steer clear of the shop. As soon as he entered the building, Moses peppered him with questions about Blessing. Barry readily supplied him with a story. He said Blessing had complained that his feet were sore and decided a trip to Barkerville was out of the question.

"That coon, I left him on the road," Barry said. Moses didn't believe him, and so when Barry returned to his shop a second time, he asked after Blessing once again. Barry repeated the same excuse. When Barry returned for a third haircut and Moses asked of Blessing's whereabouts yet again, Barry glared back at Moses and muttered angrily under his breath.

The three encounters Moses had with Barry left Moses even more concerned for his missing friend. He may not have known Blessing long, but Moses had a gift when it came to reading people. Blessing struck him as a reliable individual, and certainly not the kind of man who gave up on a quest that was so important to him. Moses mulled over the story of Blessing having sore feet long after Barry left his shop. It was a feeble excuse, Moses knew. He had a sinking feeling that all was not well with his friend. Then something happened to fuel Moses' suspicions further.

Sometime after Barry's visit, another miner showed up for a haircut. The unnamed gentleman was wearing an interesting and unique skull-shaped gold pin. It wasn't a common design, but Moses had seen one just like it on the jacket Blessing had worn. After questioning his customer, Moses learned that the miner had received the pin from a local dancehall girl. More determined than ever to find Blessing, Moses sought out the dancehall girl in question. When asked, she explained she got it from none other than James Barry as payment for services rendered. Any suspicions Moses had about Barry before were now solidified. Moses was convinced that his friend had come to harm, and he was certain Barry had something to do with it. The problem was that aside from the pin and a strong gut feeling, Moses had nothing to back his beliefs.

A few weeks later, Moses experienced something that had him doubting his concerns—and then his sanity. On a particularly slow day the door to his shop opened and the bell rang, indicating that a customer had arrived. When Moses turned to see who it was, he saw Blessing standing there. Blessing said he wanted a shave, but to Moses' way of thinking his friend needed a lot more than a shave. The man he'd met was well kempt and had a healthy glow about him. The Blessing that stood at the door to Moses' shop looked like he'd been dragged through Hell. His clothes were tattered, his hair was a matted mess, and there was a vacant look about his eyes. Moses directed the man to a chair and excused himself to get a warm towel. As he wrapped the towel around Blessing's face, he told his friend how worried he'd been about him, and how he'd planned to organize a search party to try and locate him. Blessing listened in silence. Ready to start the shave, Moses turned for his razor, but when he turned back the hot towel he'd wrapped around his friend's face appeared to be soaked in blood. Horrified, Moses lifted the towel and suddenly, there was nothing there. Blessing had evaporated into thin air.

Shaken by the experience, Moses initially wondered if he was going mad. Then he remembered how Blessing had pulled him aside before leaving Quesnel and shared his concerns about his safety. No, Moses argued with himself, he wasn't going crazy. It was Blessing's spirit that visited his shop that day, Moses was certain. Blessing was urging Moses to contact the authorities, to find his body and, if possible, to find and punish his murderer.

More determined than ever, Moses set out to find some answers. He started off by approaching the local authorities with his concerns. Of course he couldn't tell them about his strange encounter with what he knew to be his deceased friend's ghost, asking for his help. Instead, Moses mentioned the skull pin and his suspicions about Barry. He shared Barry's explanation about Blessing's absence and explained why he thought the story was so flawed.

Perhaps it was Moses' persistence, or just happenstance, but in the fall of 1866, a man's remains were discovered near Beaver Pass, between Quesnel and Barkerville, at a point where the Cariboo Wagon Road intersected an old trail. The body had reportedly been tossed carelessly in the bush and must have been there for some time because little more than a skeleton remained.

It wasn't hard to identify the remains as belonging to Charles Blessing. The clothes found by the skeleton were exactly what Moses remembered his friend wearing when he last saw him. But there was more. A news report covering the discovery described several items found on the body as having the initials C.M.B. on them, and a drinking cup identified the initials even more: it read "C.M. Blessing."

It's strange that whoever killed the man also left behind many valuable articles, among them a few grains of gold that were wrapped up in paper. They would not, however, get away with murder. Despite the condition of the body, a bullet hole through the skull left no doubt the man's death was no accident.

Moses had initially alerted the authorities about his missing friend and the person who he thought might be responsible. Now, receiving information about the discovery, Moses was determined to put the final nail in Barry's coffin. He knew that Barry owned a six-shooter, and he wasted no time in sharing that information with the authorities.

When Barry was finally arrested, he asked the officer who made the accusation against him. The officer told Barry he would soon find out, but Barry said he already knew it was Moses who had turned him in.

When the case of the murder of Charles Blessing finally made it to trial, Moses told the courts everything he knew, and how he came to his conclusions that Barry was the man behind the bullet that ended Blessing's life. But a final decision didn't rest on Moses' testimony alone. Other witnesses came forward with their own evidence against the accused. A man by the name of H.P. Stark said he had bumped into Barry at Thirteen Mile House, and at that point Barry had been travelling with a man who matched Blessing's description. Another witness named William Fraser testified that he had also travelled with Barry, and he knew Barry carried a six-shooter. Other witnesses came forward supporting Moses' description of Blessing's good character. And one George Gartley described a particular gold pin he had seen Blessing wear—the same gold pin that Moses recognized on a client as belonging to his friend.

As one witness after another took the stand, they destroyed any thread of a reasonable doubt as to Barry's guilt. Judge Matthew Begbie presided over the trial, and in August of 1867, he passed final judgment in the case, agreeing with the jury's guilty verdict. "It is impossible to conceive a crime more wanton or atrocious than that which you have committed. I can offer you no hope of mercy. You have…dyed your hands in blood, and must…suffer the same fate," Judge Begbie told Barry. "My painful duty now is to pass the last sentence of the law on you…; which is that you be taken to the place whence you came and from thence to the place of execution, there to be hanged by the neck until you are dead; and may the Lord have mercy on your soul."

For Moses, the judgment was the first step in his quest to honour his friend. His next step was to give Blessing a proper burial. Once this was accomplished, Moses felt as though he'd done all he could for his deceased friend. Blessing had reached out to Moses for help while at the same time bidding him a final farewell. Moses could now relax knowing he'd done everything he could to honour the memory of a man whose only desire was to explore this country's wild west and, with any luck at all, live to tell the tale.

Chapter 3

A Matter of Love?

~

Most of us would agree that it's flattering to know you've turned a head or two in your day. Some of us might even know what it's like to have to choose between two suitors. But it's a rare lass indeed that's stirred enough emotion in the hearts of two men to become the subject of a duel.

Such was the case for a pretty young Irish girl who lived near Quidi Vidi, which was a small fishing village at the time but is now a neighbourhood in St. John's, Newfoundland and Labrador. Captain Mark Rudkin of the British army and Ensign John Philpot, a 27-year-old member of the Royal Veteran Company, were seriously engaged in a game of cards on the evening of March 29, 1826. Several others of their company were at the table that night, too, but as the evening wore on, only Rudkin and Philpot remained.

As is usually the case in any kind of conflict, there was a bit of history between the two men. There was more than the afore mentioned matter of the young lady, though she certainly put a damper on any friendship that might have previously existed between the men. Philpot also had the unfortunate habit of letting his mouth run off uncensored and, at one point, had hurled some kind of insult at Rudkin. He later apologized, but the memory of the slight was still fresh in Rudkin's mind. Add to that the matter of the game at hand, the rum that was flowing freely, and the significant amount of money Philpot had lost at the table, and you have a sure recipe for disaster.

Rudkin and Philpot decided to play one last hand; Philpot was desperately hoping to recoup some of the money he'd lost that night. But Rudkin won that last round, and because Rudkin had dealt, Philpot naturally accused him of cheating. The disagreement escalated from an exchange of words to a tussle over the money and a swift kick to Rudkin's backside. The captain was beyond outraged. Concerned about defending his honour, which had been badly bruised in front of several of his own men, he challenged Philpot to a duel. The die had been cast.

The two men, along with their seconds, met the following morning on a field about a mile outside Quidi Vidi near an establishment called Brine's Tavern. By then the rum had worn off for Rudkin, and his temper had cooled. He was no longer interested in facing off with the young ensign, and Dr. James

Coulter Strachan, the British army surgeon who was Rudkin's second, agreed. Both men tried to talk some sense into the young man, but Philpot wasn't easily dissuaded. Captain George Farquhar Morice was Philpot's second. Even Morice, who was well aware of Rudkin's prowess with a firearm, tried his best to convince Philpot to change his mind. But Philpot was still convinced Rudkin had been cheating, and he was going to make the man pay in more ways than one. Besides, there was still the matter of the young maiden's hand to settle.

Rudkin was by far the better shot, but he wasn't interested in winning this duel with a display of his expert marksmanship. Instead, he had a plan. When the two men faced off, Rudkin had the sun at his back. The glare blurred Philpot's line of vision, and when he fired the only damage he inflicted was to nick his target's collar. Rudkin, on the other hand, could have dropped Philpot without any difficulty. Instead, the crack shot fired his gun into the air and thought that would be the end of the entire affair.

Unfortunately, Philpot was as determined as ever and demanded they go at it again. It was clear that Philpot wasn't going to give up. Knowing that Philpot, a decent shot in his own right, would eventually hit his target, Rudkin thought twice about aiming in the air that second round. This time he pointed at Philpot and pulled the trigger, hitting him just above the heart. The story goes that Philpot was ironically laid to rest in the nearby Anglican churchyard on April 1, the fool's day.

Meanwhile, Rudkin, a good man and a stalwart soldier, was troubled by the entire ordeal and reported what happened to his commanding officer. As a result, Rudkin was charged with murder, and both seconds were arrested and charged as accessories. Initially, public opinion demanded justice for Philpot, believing the man didn't stand a chance against the more experienced Rudkin. Judicial proceedings moved considerably faster back then than they do now, and once all the details were uncovered, Rudkin and the two seconds were viewed in a more compassionate light. On April 17th, a jury found all three men not guilty.

This duel is considered Canada's last deadly duel and, as would be fitting of such a tragic story, an ethereal figure believed to belong to Philpot's angry spirit has been seen in the intervening years, roaming the hillside where the duel occurred. Some suggest that the spirit doesn't belong to Philpot at all, but to another, unidentified man who met his end in an equally disturbing way. In this theory, the unnamed spirit is believed to have appeared to Rudkin and Philpot prior to the duel, warning participants of the tragedy about to unfold. Although it's an interesting suggestion, most witness reports describe the ghost as wearing a soldier's uniform with bloodstains in the chest area where Philpot was shot, suggesting that it is indeed Philpot's spirit that floats across that hillside, enraged at being beaten at cards and again in the duel and lamenting a future he never had the chance to experience with the woman he loved.

And if that weren't enough to produce a woeful afterlife, it is believed that Philpot's grave had to be exhumed during the construction of St. John's Anglican Cathedral many years later. Many spiritual perspectives would suggest that a person's soul cannot rest once his grave has been unearthed. Clearly, Philpot would have been better off had he accepted Rudkin's truce.

Chapter 4

Harbinger of Death

~

Beacon Hill Park is, according to its official website, "one of downtown Victoria's crown jewels." The 200-acre property was officially established as a park in 1882 and was named "after a pair of masts strategically placed on a hill to act as a beacon and navigational aid to mariners approaching Victoria's inner harbour." The park itself is a meticulously managed landscape of natural and manmade beauty, boasting a huge variety of exotic and native trees and attracting a wide assortment of birds and wildlife. There are walking trails throughout the park linking it to neighbouring streets, a putting green for avid golfers, a petting zoo for kids, a stage for summer concerts and even a path for horse-drawn carriages. In a nutshell, it's a little breath of fresh air in an otherwise busy metropolis. It's also home to at least one ghost.

Witnesses first reported seeing a tall, thin woman with tanned skin and long blonde hair wandering in the early morning hours near a mound of rocks amid a thicket of bushes near

Douglas and Superior streets sometime in the mid-1970s. She looked terrified, her mouth frozen in what appeared to be a silent scream and her arms raised as if she was trying to protect herself. She seemed so real that her appearance propelled some bystanders to rush over with offers of help, only to stand there confused when the woman simply evaporated into thin air. She was a ghost, it was soon realized. What other explanation could there be? But no one could determine who she was before she died. Surely someone interested in the paranormal would have attempted to channel the spirit and discover her identity. And yet her identity remained unknown.

Then just as suddenly as her appearances began, they stopped. With the exception of the people who had actually seen her, she was soon forgotten. There were no more reported sightings of the spirit with the frozen scream until 1983. Sometime that summer, people started seeing a tall, thin woman standing with her mouth gaping and arms outstretched, her eyes wide with terror. Her manner and expression were identical to the 1970s sightings, but there was a noticeable difference. Unlike the previous version, this woman had fair skin, and her long hair was dark. She was the photographic negative of her earlier incarnation.

A theory was beginning to develop. Was it possible that the phenomenon witnessed in 1983 was the ghost of a young woman who had just recently died, but the 1970s "ghost" was really its doppleganger? Literally translated from its Germanic origin, a doppleganger is a "double-walker" or "double-goer." This "alter ego" or "spirit double" is said to be a harbinger of death. Was the woman's look-alike, in some earlier, parallel reality, foretelling a tragedy that wouldn't occur until years later?

The newer version of the apparition was repeatedly seen at the same mound of rocks until later that same year. Then one afternoon in November, a park employee making his rounds discovered partially exposed human remains after a rainfall washed away the thin layer of soil covering the body. Once the authorities arrived and exhumed the shallow grave, the decomposed body of a young woman was uncovered. It had been hastily buried a stone's throw from the neighbouring walking path in an area littered by coffee cups, candy wrappers and even a discarded school book.

The remains were identified as belonging to 31-year-old Donna Mitchell—fair-skinned with long, dark hair. According to a *Times Colonist* article from September 2008, reporting on what was by then a cold case, Dave Robertson, the woman's common-law husband, had reported her missing on June 3, 1983, after she didn't show up for her seven-year-old daughter's birthday party. In the days following her disappearance, police attempted to retrace her movements. They confirmed she had been to see her doctor the day she disappeared. She had drinks with friends at the King's Hotel on Yates Street later that same day and, after that, she was spotted near the Empress Hotel. That was the last confirmed sighting of the woman, at least as far as a physical sighting goes.

Was it possible that it was Donna Mitchell's ghost calling out to people during the months prior to the discovery of her remains, begging for someone to find her and provide her with a proper burial and, if possible, to find her killer and bring him to justice? Mitchell had been strangled to death. It was horrifying to think that when people described seeing a woman whose mouth appeared to be frozen in a silent scream, they were in fact seeing Mitchell's final struggle.

Victoria police officers Sgt. Ross Swanton and Sgt. Paul Awalt began working the murder investigation by interviewing Mitchell's friends and penetrating deeper into her background. They knew she had struggled somewhat with drug use, and she had some friends with struggles of their own. Furthermore, forensic evidence had determined that Mitchell had been murdered elsewhere and her body moved to the location at Beacon Hill Park.

An undercover investigation pointed officers in the direction of one friend in particular, a transvestite prostitute who had been in the city at the time. Although details weren't released as to why he was of particular interest to police, they were collecting what they believed was enough evidence to arrest the man for murder. Unfortunately, the suspect hanged himself before that happened.

"Our suspect we figure did it, hung himself," Swanton told reporters. "We had all the evidence and everything else, but we couldn't finish it off… I think he must have known we were on to him."

Because Mitchell's death remains on the cold case files, there is a lot about it that remains shrouded in mystery. There was no suggestion that Mitchell had been a prostitute, and it's unclear how she knew the suspect. "Something just got out of hand," was all Swanton would tell reporters when they asked for a connection between the two.

Even with the death of their main suspect, Swanton and Awalt kept studying Mitchell's murder. Awalt even shared his notes on the case with Seattle detectives who, at that time, were investigating Gary Ridgway, the Green River Killer. Ridgway was eventually convicted of the murders of 49 women, but he confessed to 71 between the years of 1982 and 1998; some authorities suggest the number of murders he was responsible for could be more than 90. Although Mitchell died in Victoria, police couldn't outright dismiss the possibility that Ridgway may have done a little travelling.

When the *Times Colonist* penned their story on the cold case in 2008, a fresh pair of eyes was looking to take the investigation in an altogether different direction. Exactly what that direction might be hasn't been made public. Swanton, however, remains convinced that he and Awalt had the killer within their grasp.

There are still occasional sightings of the ghost of a woman many have come to believe was Donna Mitchell in life. However, her ghostly doppleganger hasn't reappeared. Perhaps, as Robin Skelton and Jean Kozocari suggest in their 1989 book, *A Gathering of Ghosts*, the doppleganger's job was to warn of future events. "It is hard to determine, however, whether the young woman herself, by a kind of astral projection, was foreseeing her own death, or whether, by curious twist in time, the place prerecorded a memory before the event had occurred."

It's quite likely that we will never know the answer to that question.

Chapter 5

Murder in the Badlands

~

If you've ever travelled through Alberta's Badlands, you'll no doubt agree the unique landscape is captivating. The Badlands cut a wide swath through much of southeastern Alberta and stretch slightly into Saskatchewan. The hoodoos, coulees, ravines and sand dunes that dominate much of what Travel Alberta has referred to as a "moon-like landscape" whisper of an earlier age when dinosaurs ruled.

In a 2005 *Calgary Herald* newspaper report, Trevor Kiitokii, a spokesman for Head-Smashed-In Buffalo Jump, explained the reverence the Native peoples had for the area. The "Badlands are looked at as one of the sacred places where the people, from my understanding, did not dwell, because it was the graveyard of the animals that lived there a long time ago. They knew that from stories from their ancestors...in the spiritual guidance, they were told this place was sacred."

Non-Native settlers, however, didn't share the same understanding of the place as their First Nations counterparts.

Adventurers were anxious to explore the unique landscape and quickly identified several considerable coal deposits. Coal had been mined in our Atlantic provinces since 1639, but it's a long way from Alberta to Grand Lake, New Brunswick, or Cape Breton, Nova Scotia. Discovering the coveted fuel in the western portion of this vast country would benefit everyone.

In 1910, Colonel Samuel Drumheller purchased the tract of land that now holds the city that bears his name. Within a year, mining operations started up and by 1912, the railway made its way through the area. By 1913 the Village of Drumheller was incorporated. Less than two decades later, in 1930, Drumheller boasted a population of almost 3000 residents and was officially declared a city. Several other communities were established around the same time as Drumheller, including the hamlet of Wayne.

Coal was a valuable commodity, used for cooking as well as home heating in a landscape with few trees and a climate where the winters are cold and unforgiving. About 10 kilometres southeast of Drumheller, the hillsides along the valley of the Rosebud River promised a considerable yield. By 1912, authorities from the Red Deer Coal Company had set up operations in what became the community of Wayne. Schools, a hospital, stores and even a theatre were built soon after to accommodate workers and ensure their families had all the necessities they required. The Last Chance Saloon and Rosedeer Hotel were built in 1913 and quickly became the gathering place for miners to relieve the stresses of their day.

A coal miner's life was a hard one, and though the job promised a steady income, working conditions were far from good. Despite the fact the community offered families everything they needed to enjoy life, the pay miners received for a dirty and dangerous job was far from adequate. From time to time disgruntled employees would confront their employers, asking for higher wages and improved working conditions. More often than not their requests fell on deaf ears. Having their requests ignored only angered the employees more, and eventually rumours began to circulate that efforts were underway to form a union. Of course, management always had ears close to the source, and such talk never advanced beyond the talking stage. There were ways to deal with unruly employees; hired muscle could take care of that job.

Legend suggests that the muscle mine management hired for the task were Ku Klux Klan thugs. It was their job to scout out insurgents, or communists, as they were often referred to, and teach them a lesson. This lesson would be delivered in various forms. According to one source, these unfortunates would be hauled to the top floor of the Rosedeer Hotel, likely because it was the only hotel in town, and beaten. Sometimes they'd be burned with the lit end of a cigarette, just in case the beating didn't drive the point home, and it wasn't unheard of for enforcers to tar and feather their victims.

Because these "lessons" were delivered by management muscle in the hotel, and also because frequent brawls occurred at the establishment, Rosedeer Hotel earned the unfortunate moniker, "the Bucket of Blood." But by far the most devastating situation occurred sometime in the 1920s when, once again, a disgruntled miner started making noise about the need for a union. The man in question, whose name seems to be lost in history, was captured and hauled up to that third floor room of the Rosedeer Hotel where he was beaten, and tarred and feathered.

Most victims of tar and feathering suffered severe burns and had to endure the pain of having the tar scraped off their body. In the end, their skin was raw and often got infected, but they usually recovered. The man in this story, though, died that night. The exact cause of death isn't known; he may have died because of the blows he received, or it is also possible that he was so covered in tar that his skin could not sweat and his body overheated. Regardless the cause, the man died.

Fast forward to the present. It's been said that location is everything. Unfortunately, the hamlet of Wayne didn't have location on its side. When natural gas offered homeowners a cleaner alternative, coal production fell drastically. While the population of Wayne had ballooned to 10,000 in its heyday, as the coal mines shut down, numbers rapidly dwindled. Living in Wayne wasn't a good option for families whose breadwinners had to look further afield for work. It was too far from main thoroughfares; the 11 bridges one must take to get there, bridges that today might entice tourists for a nice day trip, would have been a considerable deterrent in those days. Families began migrating to Drumheller or other communities with better work opportunities, or out of the area altogether.

Today, with about 30 residents who call Wayne home, the community can't quite be called a ghost town. On January 1, 1998, the small hamlet officially amalgamated with Drumheller. The Rosedeer Hotel, which includes the Last Chance Saloon, is the only original building that still stands in its entirety. It continues to draw visitors, standing as a testament to an earlier time in Alberta's, and Canada's, history. A boar's head stares out through an assortment of cowboy curiosities and mining paraphernalia that decorate the saloon walls. A sign that still sits on an old shuffleboard table reads, "We don't take bills larger than $2." And if you look closely, you'll find at least two bullet holes in the wall, remnants of an earlier barroom battle.

All in all, not much has changed since the Dayman family built the hotel in 1913. The décor in the hotel rooms has remained true to the building's early roots, even after the hotel changed hands for the first time a few years back. And despite the age of the facility, rooms are still offered for rent, with one exception: the third floor remains off limits to the public.

Visitors haven't been able to rent a room on that floor for some time, but the ghost of a seemingly angry man has been seen making his way up the stairs and, according to some brave souls who've dared to follow, along the third floor hallway and into that infamous room. Anyone who has seen the ghost believes it is the man who died after being tarred and feathered many years before. Enraged at the way he was treated, and furious that no one in the hotel intervened on his behalf, the man's spirit refuses to leave.

Some visitors to the hotel have reported waking in the middle of the night in their second floor room, roused by the sound of creaking overhead, as if someone was walking in the room above them. Others have reported feeling a strange presence that made them feel ill at ease.

Other ghosts circulate in the community of Wayne, too. No doubt a few of those other discontented souls lost their earthly life in some deadly form of Wild West battle or other. As former Rosedeer Hotel owner Fred Dayman once said, "the whole area is heavy with spirit." One thing is certain: the ghost at the Rosedeer Hotel isn't ready to move on to the other side any time soon.

Chapter 6

Ghost Woman
of Keenan Bridge

~

At one time there were more than 300 covered wooden bridges in the province, so it's no wonder New Brunswick was nicknamed the "Covered Bridge Province." The Keenan Bridge was among that number, spanning the Monquart River until May 3, 2001, when it went up in flames. Crowds surrounded the blazing inferno as firefighters raced to extinguish the fire and save the structure.

The fire happened just days before the nearby community of Johnville was scheduled to host its annual community picnic. Townsfolk had decided to dedicate the event to the historic bridge, which was built in 1927; now all they could do was stand by, watching smoke rise from the smouldering trusses.

An investigation into the cause of the fire suggested that it was arson, though the person or people responsible have never been identified. But there are those who have another explanation for the blaze. Some believe that the ghost of an unknown woman, unhappy with the planned celebration, destroyed the bridge. This theory is backed up by a photograph snapped by one of the townsfolk that gathered around the burning bridge; according to one source, the photo depicts the "disembodied, semi-transparent head" of a woman, hovering "over the ruins, staring directly into the camera. Her faded features were discernible enough to make out a head of dark hair, which seemed to be piled in a bun over her head, and a surprising callow complexion."

The ghost of the Keenan Bridge is an old story that dates back to the bridge's original construction. Folklore has it that one of the labourers working on the project made an astonishing discovery while preparing the ground for the bridge's overpass. While digging, the man unearthed a human skull. It was certainly disconcerting, especially given the fact that the rest of the skeleton was never discovered.

Regardless of the find, construction continued until the covered bridge was complete. The men that made up the construction crew certainly weren't the kinds of individuals that indulged in flights of fancy, but they uniformly agreed that the bridge seemed to have a disturbing aura about it. The finished structure felt dangerous somehow, like there was an evil force threatening to attack anyone who passed through.

It wasn't long before those feelings of foreboding resulted in a near miss for a local farmer returning home from a business trip in Johnville. The man was steering his horse-drawn buggy along the road up to the entrance of the bridge when, for no apparent reason, he stopped. As he peered into the covered tunnel, the man simply couldn't dismiss the discomfort he felt. It was like the bridge itself, or some entity inside the structure, was staring back at him.

The feeling unnerved him so much that he pondered turning around and going home via another bridge. But that was silly, he argued with himself. It would add considerably to his travel time, and he was tired. So he snapped his horse's reins and moved onto the wooden platform.

The sound of the hooves against the wood was deafening, echoing throughout the narrow passage, reverberating back to the man. He felt the presence of a woman and, although he couldn't see her, he had the distinct impression that she was sitting next to him. He was also convinced that she wasn't of this earthly world, and she wasn't a benevolent spirit.

As the horse and buggy came out on the other side of the bridge, the man turned and for an instant saw the woman whose presence he had felt. "She was white," he would later tell anyone who would listen. "Whiter than white, pale as a corpse or the bone of an animal. And her hair was long and straight, black as pitch and blowing all around her. She wore a heavy black dress, buttoned right up to her chin, and there was no mistaking her for anything but evil...It was in her eyes. The Devil was in her eyes. She smiled at me, and I thought I saw the Devil. I was sure I was going to die."

The farmer lived to tell the tale, but it's unlikely he ever travelled the Keenan Bridge again.

The farmer's story isn't unique. There are countless stories of the ghost woman of the Keenan Bridge appearing to travellers crossing that bridge over the years. She spooked horse and rider until motor vehicles replaced that means of travel, and then terrified motorists with her negative energy and occasionally her ethereal image.

Some reports of the ghost mirror that of the first farmer who came forward to share his experience. But other accounts are slightly different. As author Dan Asfar shared in his account of the legend, "many people claimed that a woman's bloodcurdling wail filled the tunnel just before they emerged to find themselves sitting next to the ghoulish female. Others added a disquieting detail, stating that the woman who appeared in their vehicle as they crossed the bridge was actually headless. Although she was described bereft of any vocal cords in these accounts, she never failed to issue a horrible cry before vanishing right in front of terrified witnesses."

It's a commonly held belief that the ghost is of the woman whose head was discovered when the site for the bridge was being excavated. The identity of that woman, however, is a mystery that has defied explanation for almost a century.

What sadness did that individual face during her earthly existence? Was she tortured and abused by her partner or some other family member? Or was she the unfortunate victim of a random act of violence? Could it be that the woman was murdered elsewhere and her body remained there? Regardless which explanation you prefer, there's no doubt the spirit had every reason to be angry.

Chapter 7

All in the Family

~

S everal wooden steps led to a stiff plank frame, and a noose hung from its horizontal beam. The man that would be responsible for securing this noose in place when the time came stood nearby, while a crowd of about 300 huddled in front of the walls that held this simple but sturdy wooden structure. Heads tilted back and eyes gazing upwards, those gathered shuddered, partly from the cool late autumn air but mostly from the sheer horror of what was about to occur. For this gallows was not located at ground level as were most others of its kind. Instead, it had been constructed on top of and overhanging one stone wall of the Huron County Gaol within full view of the unlucky prisoner for whom it was being built. Confined to his cell in an adjoining wing of the octagonal building, the man pondered his inevitable fate with every swing of the hammer.

Some of those huddled together in their groups on that crisp day, December 7, 1869, were outraged at what they believed to be a miscarriage of justice, heartbroken for the man whose life was about to be cut short and fearful of what they were about to see. They refused to believe that Nicholas Melady Jr. was responsible for the murder of his father, Nicholas Sr., and stepmother, Ellen, on June 6, 1868. They argued that the real murderer was still out there, and that Nicholas Jr. was just the fall guy. Others in the crowd supported the inevitable event; they believed in whatever spurious methods were allegedly used to support the man's guilty verdict and subsequent death sentence and were anxious to see the hands of justice at work.

In his book *Double Trap*, John Melady, a descendant of the unfortunate victims and the accused, explained that Nicholas Melady Sr. was a powerful man in Huron County, Ontario, and had amassed a considerable amount of real estate in the area. He wrote of how the older man wasn't very nice to his family, often pitting them against each other to acquire his wealth. According to John, the family lore suggests that Nicholas Jr. was perhaps the most abused of the family, often forced to work for no pay and told he wouldn't get a cent of inheritance when the time came.

No one could blame Nicholas Jr. for being angry with his father. After a night of drinking with his buddies, the young man seemed to have acquired some liquid courage. Accompanied by two friends, Nicholas broke in to his father's house and confronted his elder. Not one to back down, Nicholas Sr. fought back and what might have began as a hot-headed dispute ended with the death of Nicholas Sr. and his new wife. All three young men at the scene were originally arrested for the crime, but eventually Nicholas Jr.'s friends turned against him. That, coupled with the testimony of a woman who'd been planted near the young man's cell to seduce him into revealing information that would prove he was indeed responsible for the murders, was enough to result in his guilty verdict.

In the days leading up to his execution, Nicholas Jr. was housed at the Huron County Gaol. The cell was situated close to the gallows where Nicholas would breathe his last. He could hear each swing of the hammer as the carpenters built his death trap. He no doubt wondered what his life would have been like had he not decided to drown his sorrows that night. Perhaps he could have just moved away and started fresh somewhere else— somewhere where the Melady name was unknown. Sadly, all he could do was dream. There would be no fresh start, no wife and kids, no normalcy for him. The only future he had to look forward to was the date he had with a hangman.

When the time came, Nicholas Jr. made his last, long walk to the roof of the prison. He caught his breath as he felt the rope lower around his neck, and moments before he plunged through the trap door and hung over the edge of the roof, he knew all hope for a reprieve was lost. There, above a crowd of mortified bystanders, his neck snapped to one side and his body swayed against the ancient stone while his arms and legs continued to jerk violently. It is believed death by hanging was initially adopted over crucifixion by Constantine the Great as a more "humane" form of execution. Those who witnessed Melady's last conscious moments wouldn't have called his end humane. With the fracture and dislocation of the man's vertebrae, the muscles in his neck and its surrounding skin would have been all that kept his body from becoming decapitated. His heart, however, could have kept beating for up to 15 minutes, and the spasmodic jerking of his body could have continued even longer. It would have been a grisly sight.

Because there was so much tension surrounding the perceived innocence or guilt of the accused in this case, the authorities decided to execute the prisoner several hours before originally planned. The time change was probably a good decision as several thousand people showed up later that day to witness the event. Who knows what mayhem may have erupted? On the other hand, public outcry speaking out on Nicholas' behalf would have, at the very least, ensured the young man left his earthly life feeling less alone. In any case, the hanging of Nicholas Melady Jr. left such an impression on people of prominent position at the time that his was the last public execution in this country.

With such a horrific event in its past, it's no wonder that some might consider a stroll through the Huron County Gaol, which was decommissioned in 1972 and now serves as a popular local tourist attraction, an unsettling venture. Some visitors have said they felt a shiver, not unlike that of an electrical current, course through their bodies while their skin turned to gooseflesh and they felt an overall sense of unease. It is believed that the sad spirit of Nicholas Melady Jr., and others like him, still wander within the historic hallways, searching for peace or, as some might believe, looking for justice.

Others have reported a more frightening sensation when they toured the facility, suggesting that prisoners who met their fate there still remain captive within these walls, as evil as the day they were captured, ready to wail and gnash their teeth at any unsuspecting visitor.

Chapter 8

The Ghost of Marie-Josephte Corriveau

~

From the very beginning it seemed like Marie-Josephte Corriveau was the kind of woman that could overcome just about anything. She was born in the rural parish of Saint-Vallier in what was then New France to Joseph Corriveau and Francoise Bolduc, and although the couple had 10 other children, Marie was the only one to survive childhood.

At the tender age of 16, the young woman married Charles Bouchard, a farmer seven years her senior. The couple had three children. Marie-Francoise was born in 1752, quickly followed by another little girl, Marie-Angelique in 1754, and a boy, Charles, in 1757. Then the unthinkable happened. Charles Sr. died, leaving Marie-Josephte a young widow with three little ones.

Sad though she must have been, Marie wasn't about to succumb to her grief. She soldiered on and, in time, found herself another husband. There aren't any details on this second relationship. Perhaps Marie thought she had found love again, or perhaps she believed she needed a husband for her and her children to survive. Regardless the reasons for the new union, Marie married Louis Etienne Dodier on July 20, 1761.

Dodier was also a farmer, so Marie would have been accustomed to the lifestyle, and yet it seems their relationship was far from smooth. Marie's father, Joseph, was at odds with his son-in-law. Details on that tumultuous relationship aren't clear, but it is thought that Dodier was abusive to Marie. The young woman was unhappy and frightened in her new marriage.

On the morning of January 27, 1763, Marie's life took yet another turn. Louis' lifeless body was discovered in the couple's barn. Louis had received multiple head wounds, and his death was officially ruled an accident, caused by "kicks of horses' hooves." While officials were satisfied with the findings, the local rumour mill had suspicions of its own. Area residents knew there was no love lost between Joseph and Louis, and they also knew that Louis had brutalized his wife on several occasions. The authorities might have blamed Louis' death on an angry or frightened horse, but the folks of Saint-Vallier thought otherwise. They believed the man had been murdered.

Given Louis' reputation, one might question the motivation behind the public outcry, but it achieved its purpose. British military authorities in charge of maintaining the peace in the area, on hearing the rumours, reopened the case. Marie and her father were both charged with Louis' murder. On April 9, 1763, Joseph was found guilty of culpable homicide and sentenced to hang. Marie was found guilty of being an accomplice to the crime. She was sentenced to 60 lashes, and her hand was branded with the letter M for murderer. Marie's cousin, Isabelle Sylvain, who proved to be an unreliable witness at the trial, was sentenced to 30 lashes and was branded with the letter P for perjurer.

Faced with a death sentence, Joseph had a change of heart. Fear for his life outweighed love for his child, and he placed full blame for Louis' death on Marie's shoulders. Louis was a brutal man, beating his daughter repeatedly, her father explained. Finally, the young woman had had enough. Surviving as a single mother was preferable to spending the rest of her life as a punching bag. According to Joseph, Marie was driven by sheer desperation when she grabbed the hatchet perched near the family's wood stove and slammed the butt end onto the head of her sleeping husband. Two blows was all she could deliver, but it was all that was needed. The man was dead; Marie was now faced with the challenge of moving the body and somehow covering up her crime.

That's where her father came in. Joseph clamined that in one last attempt to protect his child, he moved Louis' body to the horse's stable. Joseph anticipated the man's death would be ruled accidental; he didn't foresee that public interest in the case would call that finding into question. At a second trial, Marie pleaded guilty, reiterating her father's story and explaining how terrified she was of her husband.

Given the testimony of her abuse, one might have expected Marie would receive some leniency in her sentencing. Unfortunately, that was not to be. Marie faced the hangman's noose on April 18 of that same year. Once she was declared dead, her body was placed in an iron cage on the corner of what is now Rue St-Joseph and the Boulevard de l'Etente and put on public display to decompose. This morbid practice was used in both England and France, presumably as a deterrent to anyone contemplating murder. By the end of May, due to public pressure from neighbouring residents, the cage was taken down. It was buried in the St-Joseph-de-la-Pointe-Levy church cemetery.

In 1849, workers digging a pit in that area of the cemetery accidentally exhumed the cage, which, oddly enough, found its way down to the church basement. Stranger still is the fact that someone was brazen enough to steal the gibbet and eventually sell it to P. T. Barnum, who used it as one of his macabre displays. It was at one time displayed at the Boston Museum and is now part of the museum collection at the Château Ramezay in Montréal, though it is currently in storage. There's no clear indication of what became of Marie's remains.

Marie's story so intrigued anyone who heard it that it seemed to take on a life of its own. Following her death, residents began to wonder if she'd also murdered her first husband; one source points out there are no concrete records of the man's death, which may have fuelled those rumours. Over time, an oral tradition has developed that has Marie with as many as seven husbands, each of whom she is said to have murdered.

With such a tortured life and horrible end, it's no wonder the spirit of Marie-Josephte Corriveau is said to haunt that busy intersection to this day. Legend has it that the spirit of "La Corriveau" returns to that cage every October 31.

Whether you believe in ghosts or not, the tragic tale of Marie-Josephte Corriveau continues to live on. Canada Post immortalized her story in September 2015 when it was chosen as one of five ghost stories in the country's second Haunted Canada stamp issue. Canada Post chose the woman because, as they explain, "her soul was said to walk the road at night, approaching travellers and grabbing anyone passing by with her claw-like hands as she opened her blood-red eyes."

Chapter 9

Murdered Innocence

~

The community of Miramichi might be the largest city in the northern part of New Brunswick, but it's by no means a metropolitan centre. It was officially formed through the amalgamation of the towns of Newcastle and Chatham in 1995 and is home to a modest population of around 12,000. But the history of European settlement in the entire Miramichi River Valley, which includes the current city, dates back to the 1700s, when the area was still home to the Mi'kmaq. By 1765 the first French communities had formed. Scottish, Irish and Loyalist immigration followed soon after, accompanied by the conflicts that often arise when new people move into a previously occupied area. But long before those bloody battles erupted, unleashing all manner of unsettled spirits to roam this part of Canada's Atlantic region, a disturbingly sinister event occurred that took the life of an innocent nun.

The story goes that Sister Marie Inconnue (also referred to as Sister Marie Unknown, as *inconnue* is French for "unknown") was a woman of impeccable honour. It's widely believed that she was the youngest daughter of a noble family and hailed from the area of Beauzeville-la-Guerard in France. At that time it was customary for the youngest daughter to consider entering religious life, which was something Marie wholeheartedly embraced. In doing so, she would have received training as a teacher and nurse to equip her for a wide variety of mission work, which she would undertake wherever her superiors deemed suitable to send her.

Obligations aside, Sister Marie was earnest in her calling. She understood herself to be the hands and feet of Jesus in the world, and she loved all the people who came into her care. And when she learned of how the Acadians living in the newly settled area of Canada were suffering and how they desperately needed schools and medical facilities, she begged her superiors to consider sending her there. Although she was gentle by nature, Sister Marie was no wallflower. She was fierce in her conviction and fearless, even in the prospect of venturing out into what most would agree was still very much a wild frontier.

Her devotion to her faith and vocation didn't go unnoticed, and she rapidly earned the respect of her superiors. It was because of her steadfast nature that she was able to convince those superiors to send her from the relative comforts of life in France to the untold hardships she would face on the rugged eastern shores of Canada in 1750. But Sister Marie survived; she even thrived in her new position. Several years later, in 1755, she met Charles Deschamps de Boishébert, a leader in the Acadian militia and a member of the Compagnies Franches de la Marine. In July 1756, with guidance from Boishébert, Sister Marie moved to a community on Beaubears Island.

Ownership and political control of this still unsettled land remained a volatile situation. Hostilities raged between the English and Acadians, and if the Acadians weren't struggling to stay alive in battle, they were fighting disease. Many men died, leaving a wake of defenceless widows and children behind. These women feared for their safety; at the very least they worried the British soldiers would rob them of whatever valuables they might have that could provide them and their children with any measure of financial security. One historical source suggests that Sister Marie helped gather these valuables to hide them in a secure place until the situation had settled. With the collection of belongings secured inside a trunk, two widows were chosen to accompany Sister Marie who, under the cover of darkness, buried it in a secret location. Unfortunately, the two widows succumbed to scurvy and died not long after, leaving Sister Marie as the sole person who knew of the treasure's whereabouts.

Some variations of this legend suggest that the treasure actually belonged to Sister Marie, or at the very least contained some of her own financial resources. This version suggests that Sister Marie was provided with the funds required to meet her own needs as well as the needs of the people she was caring for. Beacause she was a young woman who could be physically overpowered by any man who chose to confront her, she didn't keep that kind of cash, or those types of valuables, on hand. And with no banking establishments in the new community in which she served, Sister Marie needed to figure out her own way of keeping that money safe. In this rendition of the legend, Sister Marie buried the valuables at a safe and discrete location and did not disclose their whereabouts to another living soul.

No matter which version is closer to the truth, one thing was certain—Sister Marie wasn't in any hurry to share the location of the chest with anyone, regardless the threat she might face. She would never betray the trust of the people under her care or risk losing the resource entrusted to her by the church.

The exact night of her death isn't known, but it's believed that the event occurred late one night in the late 1750s. Sister Marie was returning to the Acadian settlement at French Fort Cove after spending considerable time in a nearby Mi'kmaq village. A young mother was in childbirth, but after labouring many hours on her own it was clear she was in trouble. She needed medical intervention, and it was her good fortune that Sister Marie was available. Without hesitation, Sister Marie had rushed to the young woman's side. For hours she soothed and coached the young mother until, after hours of difficult labour, she finally guided a healthy new life into the world. It was as exhilarating an experience as it was exhausting. The new mother was spent, but thanks to Sister Marie she would recover. Leaving mother and child to rest and bond, Sister Marie headed back to her camp.

Despite all the brutality she had experienced since arriving in Canada, Sister Marie had once again witnessed the miracle of birth. As tired as she was, she cherished the experience and as she walked, she relived the events of the previous few hours. Consumed in thought, Sister Marie may not have been as aware of her surroundings as she should have been.

There are several versions of the altercation that led to her gruesome death. One story tells of how a mad trapper attacked Sister Marie out of sheer rage or whim as she crossed the bridge spanning Crow Brook. For no apparent reason this mad trapper pounced on the defenceless nun, cutting her head off and running with it back into the forest, leaving her body behind.

Another tale finds Sister Marie confronted by two sailors who'd been stricken by leprosy and gone mad. In a frantic attempt to escape their confines and sail back home, the two men challenged the young woman, demanding she reveal the location of the money (or treasure) in question. When she refused to provide her attackers with the information they were looking for, they beat her. When that didn't produce the results they expected, one of the attackers, in a frenzied and violent rage, grabbed his sword and swung at her neck, decapitating the helpless woman. It's unclear why, but one of the sailors supposedly grabbed the woman's hair to lift the head from the ground and look into her face. It's said that the men were so horrified by the expression of pain on Sister Marie's face that they tossed the head over the bridge out of reflex, and ran. They were never found.

Although two sailors may have attacked Sister Marie in an effort to collect the hidden treasure, it's doubtful they were lepers because the first cases of leprosy in Canada were recorded much later, in the 1800s. Nonetheless, regardless of who was responsible for Sister Marie's ruthless murder, her body was discovered by French troops the next day. Her head, however, was nowhere to be found. Even after a troop of soldiers conducted a lengthy search of the area, her head wasn't recovered. Great care was taken to prepare what remained of the nun's body for its return to France, where it was interred.

As horrible as her death must have been, the fact that her head was never recovered was even more tragic for Sister Marie's soul. In the Catholic tradition, respect for a deceased's body is crucial, and its burial represents the hope of the resurrection. An afterlife without one's head is unthinkable. And so Sister Marie's spirit is said to wander the shores of French Fort Cove, searching the waters that flow beneath the Crow Brook bridge in search of her head. Her ethereal form has been spotted by countless witnesses, many of who have admitted conversing with the desperate spirit who, on occasion, has even offered a reward for the right information. Should you want to catch a glimpse of the headless nun for yourself, it is said the best time to explore the area is on a full moon.

More than 300 years have passed since Sister Marie met her unfortunate end, and yet her story remains ingrained in local history. Treasure hunters still scour the area where, some believe, an undiscovered treasure remains hidden. One man thought he hit the mother lode when, under a full moon, the spade he was using hit something that sounded metallic. He was sure he'd finally found the missing treasure, but before he had the chance to lift his spade again, a blur of white rushed past him. He knew instinctively it was Sister Marie's ghost protecting her stash all these centuries later. Frightened, the man ran to safety, but when he returned the next day, he was unable to locate the spot where he'd been digging.

To date, his story represents the closest anyone has come to finding the chest the good sister is believed to have buried. Sister Marie's ghost continues to make its rounds.

Chapter 10

The Hanging Tree

~

Ghostly sightings and chilling occurrences surrounding the places where hangings have taken place aren't uncommon. In fact, these eerie manifestations have done their part in keeping the memories of long-ago events alive.

Such was the case in the story of Peter Cartell. The *History of the Court of Chancery in Nova Scotia* recounts how Peter Cartell stabbed Abraham Goodside, along with two other men. All four men worked aboard the immigrant ship *The Beaufort,* which had set anchor only days before in the large cove outside of what would become the city of Sydney, Nova Scotia. There are no details explaining what the argument was about, but Goodside received a long gash in the altercation. He died instantly, and Cartell was arrested for his murder.

A document published by Acadia University in Nova Scotia described how Cartell was tried in an empty warehouse on the waterfront two days after Goodside's murder. A jury of his peers heard Cartel's case and on August 31, 1749, found him guilty. Historical sources differ somewhat as to the date Cartel was hanged; some suggest the man met his fate on September 2 while others report it was on September 13. In any case, in keeping with the tradition of the day, a large tree was chosen to serve as a gallows. The hangman's noose was tossed over a sturdy branch of the tree, which stood where, generations later, Bedford Row and George Street would intersect. In this spot, Cartell breathed his last.

The case surrounding Cartel's murder conviction and subsequent execution went down in history as the "first order of business" for the first General Court established in the new colony. But Cartel was not the last criminal whose case was heard by this new court, nor was he the only convicted criminal sentenced to hang from the makeshift gallows. What became known as the "hanging tree" was used for more than a decade before it was cut down in 1763.

The site where this bit of legal history occurred looks nothing like it did back in the mid-1700s. However, echoes of those early years still appear from time to time. Local lore suggests that on certain nights, when the moon is spilling just the right amount of light, you can see the body of a young man hanging by his neck and swinging in the breeze near the George Street intersection where the hanging tree had been located. Could this be the ghost of Peter Cartel? Or could it belong to one of the other convicted criminals who died while dangling from the limbs of that tree?

The junction of George Street and Bedford Row is just one of many stops during the Ghosts & Legends of Historic Sydney tour. If you're ever visiting the area you may want to go for an evening stroll, especially if there happens to be a full moon, and see if you can catch a glimpse for yourself.

Chapter 11
Friends and Rivals

~

The evils of alcohol have led to the demise of many a man, so it's no surprise that when two young ladies downed a couple of bottles of whisky, there were deadly consequences.

Life was tough for Irish immigrants back in the 1870s, especially in the area of Griffintown, Montréal. The working-class neighbourhood was originally established in the 1820s around the harbour front of Lachine Canal. Griffintown was an industrial hub with breweries, foundries, flour mills and other factories providing employment to many of the Irish immigrants fleeing the potato famines in their own country and settling in the growing city.

But all was far from perfect. Although the factories provided employment, working conditions were poor, and there simply weren't enough jobs to meet the needs of an ever-burgeoning population. As a result, most of the people living in Griffintown at the time struggled to provide for the basic necessities of life, and many residents suffered from disease and malnutrition. Simply put, the future wasn't much more promising for a good number of those residents than it had been in their homeland, and Griffintown would become known as one of this country's first industrial slums.

Mary Gallagher and Susan Kennedy were two young women trying to survive in that tumultuous time in Griffintown's history. With jobs available to only the strongest of men, and without a husband or family to lean on, the future for both women looked bleak. Prostitution was one of the few ways women could earn a living and, sadly, both Mary and Susan had long since turned to that trade as a means of survival. Those who knew Mary and Susan recalled them being the best of friends. They lived together, and they worked the streets together. For the most part they had each other's back, but where business was concerned, that friendship was frequently tested.

Mary wasn't necessarily prettier than Susan, but she was allegedly better at attracting the opposite sex. Not only did she have more customers and, therefore, more money than Susan, she also quite possibly attracted, shall we say, a better class of clientele. It seems that Susan, though frustrated with Mary's success, coped with it until the night of June 27, 1879. The women had met a young, good-looking man named Michael Flanagan at a local bar where they'd been downing their whisky. After a few drinks, the party moved to the girls' flat on the corner of William and Murray streets. Both women were eyeing the attractive Flanagan with the goal of having a few laughs and making a few bucks along the way. Making a living by selling your body was one thing, but a nice piece of eye candy like Flanagan certainly made the job easier.

Flanagan was having a good time enjoying the attention of two women, but he definitely preferred Mary to Susan. Unfortunately, Mary's apparent conquest also served as the nail in her coffin.

Intoxicated beyond reason and possessed by an ever-escalating jealousy, Susan grabbed the axe the women kept in the apartment to chip kindling for the stove. Without hesitation she slammed it into her best friend.

In an instant Mary was dead—decapitated, in fact. Her blood was splattered throughout the apartment and all over her attacker. In a last act of barbarity, Susan grabbed Mary's head by its blood-soaked hair and tossed it into the water bucket the women kept beside the stove.

It's unclear when Susan regained any level of sobriety, but chances are that when she did, she most likely noticed that Flanagan had passed out and slept through the entire ordeal. The apartment looked like it had been bathed in blood. What on earth had she done?

Both Susan and Flanagan were taken into custody for Mary's murder. A bewildered Flanagan was quickly released because, although the apartment was covered in blood, he was not. Susan, on the other hand, was dripping with the evidence of her crime. She was found guilty and sentenced to hang on December 5, 1879. Prime Minister Sir John A. Macdonald is credited with converting the woman's death sentence to life in prison just in time to save her life.

After 16 years behind bars, Susan was paroled. In an odd twist of fate, Michael Flanagan drowned in the Lachine Canal on the exact day of Susan's original death sentence, which some might say is proof positive that it's bad manners to fall asleep on a lady. Perhaps the spirit of Mary Gallagher had a hand in the man's death.

Mary would find no peace following her friend's guilty verdict. Mary had died a vicious and painful death, and her spirit couldn't rest. It's not clear when the first stories of a ghostly apparition in Griffintown began circulating, but tales of a woman's ghost wandering in the area were popular between 1886 and 1928. In time witnesses began to notice that sightings of the spirit coincided with the date of Mary Gallagher's death. Sometimes the ghost looked like a normal, full-bodied woman, and at other times it looked like a woman without a head. Regardless of its appearance, what became known as the ghost of Mary Gallagher always seemed to be looking for something— her head, most assumed. Although her head was discovered at the scene of the crime and buried with the rest of her remains, it seems her spirit could never reconnect the two parts of her brutalized body.

Legends flex and transform, sometimes with every telling, and the story of Mary Gallagher is a prime example of such a metamorphosis. While some tales say that Gallagher's ghost has been seen regularly over the years since her death, other stories suggest it first made an appearance on the seventh anniversary of Mary's murder and has reappeared every seven years since. Because of that, June 27 became known as Mary Gallagher Day in Griffintown.

Althought some people still report seeing what they believe to be Mary Gallagher's ghost, others suggest she stopped making herself known in 1928 after the apartment building where the crime occurred was torn down. Regardless, paranormal specialists and ghost-hunters alike have returned to the Griffintown location on seven-year anniversary dates as recently as 2012, trying to catch a glimpse of the ghost of Mary Gallagher and maybe, just maybe, bring her some measure of peace.

If you're inclined to hunt for the ghost of Mary Gallagher, the next seven-year anniversary of her death is June 27, 2019.

Chapter 12

Mobster Princess
Haunts Museum

~

The eight heritage buildings that comprise the Fort Saskatchewan Museum and Historic Site (FSMHS) occupy a parcel of land near Legacy Park, Fort Saskatchewan, Alberta. Among the permanent exhibits is Castle School (built in 1902), Dr. Henry's residence (1913), a Court House (1909), the Kulak Home (1905), Soda Lake Church (1911), a blacksmith shop and machine shed, the original North West Mounted Police Fort (1875–1885), the warden's house (1937) and a jail exhibit. The buildings are arranged to form a "picturesque historic village serenely overlooking the North Saskatchewan River," as the museum's website aptly describes it. But the quaint reminder of the early days of this sunshine province can't completely eliminate the dark clouds that are part of any community. Maintaining law and order has always been a challenge, no matter where or during what era a person lives, and the site of the FSMHS once served as law and order central for a large portion of the province. According to one researcher,

29 people were hanged between 1916 and 1960 at the jail on that site. Many of those executions were controversial, but perhaps none more so than that of Mary Florence Lassandro.

Florence was born Filomena Costanzo, but she changed her first name to fit in better in her new Canadian home. "The Mobster Princess," as some historians have nicknamed 22-year-old Lassandro, and her husband, Carlo, were Italian immigrants who were employed by a rum-running godfather named Emilio Picariello. Picariello, who also went by the moniker "Emperor Pic," was actually quite the popular guy in the town of Blairmore, in the Crowsnest Pass. Along with his illegal exploits, Picariello owned a hotel there, and also served as a town councillor.

At least one source pegs Lassandro as an abused wife who was forced into an unhappy marriage at the age of 15. For the most part, she simply did what she was told or suffered the consequences. In any case, her marriage led to her involvement with Picariello and began her life of crime.

Rum running during prohibition might have paid well, but a life of crime never has a happy ending.

There are differing stories about what led to the hangman's noose for Lassandro and Picariello. One variation of the tale has the pair entering Alberta from British Columbia in September 1922 when officers attempted to serve the godfather with a warrant. Rare is the mob boss who'd roll over and simply accept the arrest, and Picariello was no exception. He tried to make his getaway, and a high-speed chase ensued. In the process, police constable Stephen Lawson fired shots at Picariello's son, who'd fled in a separate vehicle. One of the bullets hit its target, but the young man was hit in the hand. In this version of the story Picariello wasn't aware of the extent of his son's injuries and feared the worst. Thinking his son had been mortally wounded, Picariello hunted Lawson down and killed the officer.

Another adaptation of that fateful night has Lassandro and Picariello riding together to make it look like they were a couple out for a typical Sunday drive. In this version, Lassandro's sole purpose for being with Picariello was to act as a decoy for a shipment of rum that was being smuggled from BC to Alberta. Picariello's son was driving the car with the smuggled goods and, as in the other version of the story, was shot in the hand. Picariello and Lassandro made their way to Lawson's home to confront the man after the shooting. What happened next is unclear. Some suggest that Lawson and Picariello were struggling over a gun when it discharged, killing the officer; others suggest that Picariello shot the man in the back after the two had words and Lawson turned to go into his house. The only indisputable facts in the scenario are that Lawson lay dead, and Lassandro and Picariello were at the scene. The pair was apprehended the next day, and surprisingly Lassandro confessed to pulling the trigger.

Looking back on the case, one would have to admit Lassandro's confession was full of holes. There was no indication the woman was capable of delivering the fatal gunshot, and even if she was, what would have been her motive? Also, if the reason for chasing down Lawson was payback for what Picariello believed was a fatal injury to his son, it would make sense that Picariello would have wanted to deliver that fatal bullet himself.

Regardless who pulled the trigger, Picariello and Lassandro were both arrested for Lawson's murder. They were found guilty and were sentenced to hang.

Realizing she wouldn't escape the hangman's noose just because she was a woman, Lassandro revealed the motive behind her confession as her execution date neared. Pleading for clemency, she wrote a telegram to the Minister of Justice, explaining that she took responsibility for the murder under direction from Picariello.

"We agreed that it would be best for me to take the responsibility and say that I did it, as women don't hang in Canada and he would get off," she was reported saying. In addition, Picariello allegedly promised the young woman that he'd take care of her family while she was in jail. "I am positive that I never had a gun in my hands…I never shot a gun in my life— [I was] always afraid of them."

Lassandro's pleas went all the way up to the Supreme Court of Canada. They all fell on deaf ears, as did the many letters to newspapers and petitions gathered by a public that seemed to be outraged that our civilized country would find it necessary to hang a woman. Strangely, the controversy didn't centre around doubt as to whether or not Lassandro was guilty of the murder, as she'd originally confessed; it focused on the fact she was a woman, and a woman shouldn't hang.

Requesting clemency based on her gender wasn't a good argument for Lassandro at a time when women had just earned the right to vote and were fighting for equality with men. Another strike against Lassandro's quest for leniency was her involvement with organized crime; it certainly cast doubt as to her innocence. Emily Murphy, the first female magistrate in the entire British Empire, and who was serving in Edmonton at the time, spoke out vehemently about the case.

"I…desire to protest against the pernicious doctrine that because a person who commits a murder is a woman that person should escape capital punishment," Murphy wrote in a letter to Prime Minister William Lyon Mackenzie King. "As women we claim the privileges of citizenship for our sex, and we accordingly are prepared to take upon ourselves the weight of the penalties as well."

The very public debate on whether to hang Lassandro or not did not end in the young woman's favour. Speaking on behalf of the legal authorities of the day, Justice Walsh stated that he certainly didn't recommend commutation for Lassandro, adding that the only point she had in her favour was that she was a woman.

"Why do you hang me when I didn't do anything?" Lassandro reportedly asked the crowd as she stood on the scaffold awaiting her fate. "Is there not anyone who has any pity?" When no one answered, she simply added: "I forgive everybody."

Many will attest to the fact that forgiveness doesn't always wash away the hurt someone experiences when they are wronged. Is it possible the spirit of Florence Lassandro still roams the land where, many years before, she breathed her last and made history as the first woman in Alberta to be hanged?

At least one employee of the FSMHS is inclined to believe Lassandro's spirit may still be lurking on the premises.

Darlene Briere was once the program coordinator with the FSMHS and has shared her paranormal experiences with several reporters over the years. One particular eventful night occurred during a Halloween sleepover in 2000. Briere had arranged a "Fright Night" for about two dozen children aged 8 to 12. In addition to the haunted house that was usually planned for Halloween nights, Briere arranged a number of games and activities to heighten the spine-chilling feel of the night.

Before turning in for the night, Briere ordered the children to grab their flashlights. It was just before midnight, the perfect time to do a security check of the grounds. The children followed Briere as she walked around the property. One of Briere's many volunteers had dressed in black and was playing the role of a boogeyman, hiding in the bushes and ready to pounce on any unsuspecting child that wandered too close. Another volunteer acted the role of fortune teller.

As the children ran off the last bit of their energy, Briere snapped photos of the flurry of activity. Some of the pictures would serve as a record of the event for the museum, but Briere thought it would also be nice to include a picture or two in each of the kids' take-home goodie bags. As the children settled down for the night, Briere and a volunteer sat in the office next door downloading the photos onto the computer.

As the women went about their task, they noticed a bright flash coming from the bathroom across the hall. "The caretaker had covered the bathtub in there with plywood in order to store things on it," Briere told author Barbara Smith. "Suddenly, as we watched, the bathtub lit up like a camera flash."

The experience spooked both women; they felt a sudden chill, and the hair on the back of their necks felt like it was standing up. Still, they had a museum full of sleeping children to mind, so they continued downloading their photos and, not perceiving any real threat, tried to push the incident to the back of their minds.

As the two women sorted through the photographs they noticed something Darlene certainly hadn't noticed when she snapped the pictures. In one of the photos there appeared to be a translucent image of a woman dressed in a long dress, standing in front of the ethereal figure of a small child. It almost looked like the child was trying to hide behind the woman. Darlene rechecked the images to see if there was any other evidence of a paranormal nature and sure enough, she found a second photo with what looked like the ghostly image of a woman's head.

The images on the photographs, the strange flash of light from the bathroom, and the cold spots wafting through the building already had Darlene on edge, but she was about to come up against a very flustered volunteer. Darlene's friend had gone upstairs to check on the girls and returned very agitated. "When she came back downstairs, she was just white. She told me, 'There's something up there. It's really cold, and the blind moved.'"

When Darlene checked the situation for herself, she agreed with her friend's assessment. "It was frightening and exciting at the same time, but there was never any feeling of danger…It was wonderful, though, to have someone there with me for collaboration."

Looking back on the history of the property that is now the museum, Darlene was convinced the ghost she saw was the spirit of Florence Lassandro. Lassandro was hanged for a crime she may not have committed, spurring her on to an afterlife of torment, tied to the place she fought so hard to leave. But there are others convicted of the same crime who were hanged there as well. Those in tune with the world of spirits believe some of their souls wander the area, too.

Robert Cook was a 22-year-old man convicted of murdering his father, step-mother and five step-siblings. He too had a date with the hangman's noose, and he also made history. Cook was the last man hanged in Alberta; he also protested his innocence to the end.

Shirley MacLeod, her husband Kent and their daughter Elizabeth were part of a tour of the jail. On their way to the room where death-row inmates were kept, Shirley pointed out the only window in the room was small, but it looked out at the gallows.

"On our way, the tour guide pointed out the stairway leading to the gallows outside. A space beside that gallows staircase was partially lit from lights we had turned on along our way. An ordinary kitchen chair sat in the corner. Liz and

I noticed a person huddled on the floor in the corner behind the chair." Then as soon as it appeared, the image faded.

Shirley asked her daughter what she saw, just to be sure the two saw the same thing. Her daughter said, "There was a guy in the corner but he disappeared."

When Shirley reported the sighting to the tour leader he wasn't surprised. Everyone who'd ever walked through the area agreed it had an eerie feel about it, he explained. In fact, workers at the site had grown so accustomed to seeing ghosts they were surprised when they didn't see one.

Is the ghost of Robert Cook also destined to roam for all eternity the place where he died?

Even though much time has passed since the jail was in use, the oppression the inmates would have felt to find themselves incarcerated there and, perhaps, put on death row is still very palatable. Don't be surprised if a visit to the FSMHS leaves you with goose bumps and has the hairs on the back of your neck standing up on end.

Chapter 13

When Push Comes to Shove

~

The *Newmarket Era: North York Intelligencer and Advertiser* called it one of the most "deliberate attempts at murder that had ever shocked the community." At around 9:30 AM, on January 5, 1876, a butcher named Michael McConnell attacked Nelson Mills. Mills was a well-respected member of his community. McConnell was a butcher who had a stall at the Hamilton Market and rented his home from Mills. The impetus for the attack was the $14 McConnell owed Mills for the month's rent.

It wasn't so much the money that was the issue for McConnell. The butcher simply refused to pay his rent until his landlord replaced the dilapidated fence around the family's home. Mills refused to replace the fence and instead issued a distress warrant against McConnell. Simply put, a distress warrant is a legal document that allows an officer to seize a tenant's property if the tenant does not pay his rent.

It was McConnell's wife who was presented with this document, and of course she panicked. Thinking she and the family were about to be tossed out of their home, she hastened over to the market to let her husband know what happened. McConnell was furious. He grabbed one of his large butcher knives and a sharpening stone and honed the blade until it gleamed.

The husband and wife were then seen walking to Mills' home, on the corner of Queen and George streets. They knocked on the door and demanded to see their landlord. Words were exchanged, followed by a struggle between the two men. For some reason Mills left his home and crossed the street, perhaps in an effort to steer the obviously enraged McConnell away from Mills' family. After Mills crossed the street, McConnell slammed the butcher knife across Mills' head and then into his side. Mills struggled to get help, screaming as he stumbled down the street, but McConnell followed, swinging his knife. He stabbed Mills several times more, in the head, back and side, before he finally stopped, stood up and calmly wiped the dying man's blood from the butcher knife.

Mills' wife and servant rushed to his side, having witnessed the entire scene. Another man had witnessed the brutal attack, as well, and had fetched the police. Detective McPherson arrested McConnell before he finished washing the blood splatter from his skin. According to the article, McConnell told McPherson that he "had done the deed in a passion, and did not know what I was doing, but that Mills had tried to injure me by turning me out of house and home." With that, McConnell handed the officer the knife, still bloody, along with a revolver he'd been carrying. Mills died from his injuries four days later. At that point McConnell was charged with murder. Strangely, there's no information on what Mrs. McConnell did when her husband snapped.

Following the attack, *The Spectator* reported: "There had been many serious crimes in Hamilton before, but the event of the attack on Nelson Mills by one of his tenants, Michael McConnell, was so brazen, violent and senseless that the community was deeply disturbed." His actions were certainly not the actions of a sane individual.

McConnell's lawyer, John Crerar, defended his client on the grounds of insanity; it was the first time in Canada's history where such a defence was presented. Crerar supported his argument by presenting witnesses who testified that McConnell had never been a violent man. However, they also pointed out that the man's disposition had changed after he'd suffered a "severe blow to the head." After that, things irritated the man quicker than usual, and he didn't seem able to act in his usual, level-headed manner.

Despite Crerar's efforts, McConnell was found guilty of the murder of Nelson Mills. Two months after the murder, the McConnell case made history for a second time when he became the first prisoner to be hanged in the Barton Street Jail. As if McConnell's story isn't strange enough, it is here, in this penal institution, where it hits an even stranger note. It seems McConnell's spirit refuses to leave.

Author Barbara Smith notes one of the first reports of a haunting at the Barton Street Jail made the front page of the January 12, 1884, edition of *Toronto World*. The article explains that prior to McConnell's execution, he was held in a cell known as the "black hole." As the name would suggest, he was isolated from the general population and placed in a small, dark room under high security—certainly not the kind of place anyone would want to be imprisoned. And yet this is where the man's spirit returns time and time again. Other prisoners did everything they could to avoid being placed in that cell, and not just because of its size and isolation. According to the article, the men were terrified of being locked behind that door because "the ghost of the man who was hanged on the wild March morning" still haunts that cell and had also been seen flitting "from room to room" and tramping "up and down the long corridor with a ceaseless stride."

With every passing year McConnell's presence became louder and more insistent, especially around the anniversary of his death. Some prisoners reported seeing what appeared to be a vision of McConnell's hanging near the black hole and adjoining corridor. They described the scene as that of a "ghostly figure with a black cap on top [falling] through a trap door and [dancing] for a minute in mid-air. Then all is still. The figure straightens out and death claims its own." The sightings were so frequent and so real that they could make even the most seasoned criminal weep like a child, and inmates would reportedly consent to any kind of punishment to avoid being locked in that cell.

Although I've not been able to dig out any evidence of prison administrators going on record to confirm that there was any merit behind the legend of McConnell's ghost, it makes sense that a man who may have had a severe brain injury could have snapped under the pressure. Maybe, just maybe, the damage went even deeper, following him to death and beyond.

And to think it all happened because of $14.

Chapter 14

The Brothers Grim

~

The future for two brothers from Fredericton, New Brunswick, should have held nothing but promise. Instead, a conviction of cold-blooded murder was the catalyst behind the execution by hanging of 22-year-old Rufus Hamilton and his brother, 23-year-old George Hamilton.

Pure greed seems to have been the impetus for the murder of 34-year-old taxi driver Norman Philip Burgoyne. Burgoyne was an independent businessman, running a two-car operation called Rideout Taxi Company from his Fredericton home. Burgoyne purchased the company sometime in the latter half of 1948. Looking to provide for his family and create his own future, Burgoyne relished the opportunity to be his own boss and, with any luck at all, grow his business as the population around him was growing. By December of that same year Burgoyne purchased a second vehicle; the 1949 Ford Custom Fordor sedan added a spot of luxury to his operation.

Burgoyne responded to his last, fatal call after having supper with his wife and three children on the night of Friday, January 7, 1949. It was about 8:15 PM when Norman's wife, Irene, answered the phone. The caller was requesting a cab at the Royal Canadian Legion. While the family settled in to enjoy a quiet evening, Norman left to pick up his fare. His two girls, aged nine and six, and his seven-year-old son would have preferred to have their dad stay home, but even in 1949, Friday could be the busiest night of the week. Duty called, and Norman happily kissed his wife goodbye and promised to return as soon as he could.

At first, Irene wasn't overly worried when the evening dragged on and Norman hadn't returned home. But as more time passed she knew that even an out-of-town dash wouldn't have delayed her husband so long. By Saturday morning, she put a call in to the police. Norman's body wasn't discovered until Monday, when his cab was reported parked on a rural road outside of town. Police discovered the man's bloodied body wrapped in a blanket and stuffed into the trunk of his newest investment. When his body was examined, the cause of death was immediately clear; someone had bashed in his skull with a blunt object. The Rolex watch he so proudly wore, valued at about $95, was missing, as was approximately $200 in cash Irene claimed her husband was carrying.

It didn't take the authorities long to pick up Rufus and George Hamilton for questioning, along with a younger unnamed brother. The youngest brother was quickly released. But the case against Rufus and George was pretty airtight, especially given the fact that George was only too willing to throw Rufus under the bus with a tale that had enough holes in it to convince police of George's guilt as well. It was clear that the brothers meant to rob Burgoyne, and they'd been planning their attack for some time. The brothers had ridden with Burgoyne on previous occasions, so the cab driver likely recognized his clients and wouldn't have felt any danger. Sadly, it was a mistake that cost the man everyone called "Sliver" his life. Burgoyne was murdered in Barker's Point, an area that has since earned the nickname Hammertown; the men who committed the crime are also frequently referred to as the Hammer Brothers.

No one can deny the brutality of this crime, nor the guilt of the parties involved. However, it would be remiss of me to omit a backstory that, while it doesn't excuse the perpetrators, does shed a little light on what might have led to the crime. George Elliott Clarke, a descendant of the Hamilton brothers, researched and wrote a book of poems and a novel based on this sad page in his family's history. The Hamilton brothers were of Mi'kmaq and African heritage, and were raised in what Clarke describes as "the dirt-poor settlement of Barker's Point." The brothers were themselves victims of violence who turned to violence to survive. That said, there is some evidence that they didn't set out to kill their victim. Their initial intent was to knock Burgoyne unconscious and rob him, but the end result was far more heinous, especially for the poor man's family.

Rufus and George were tried separately, and both were found guilty of murder; it seems the lesser crime of manslaughter was not considered. The Hamilton brothers died at the end of a hangman's noose in the early morning of July 27, 1949. As the *Telegraph Journal* stated, "when George and Rufus were hanged the roofs were crowded. There were kids and young adults perched on those roofs like...black birds around a pea patch all waiting for this moment."

No one emerged victorious from this crime. The Burgoyne children lost their father, and the spirits of the Hamilton brothers, as unsettled in death as they were in life, are still seen on occasion, wandering the streets of Fredericton. Some witnesses have caught glimpses of the boys ducking into back alleys. Others have come forward to report two ghostly figures sauntering down the road at night and even on occasion trying to hitch a ride. With the story of the Hammer Brothers still very much part of Fredericton's historic culture, you can bet no one stops to offer them a lift.

Chapter 15

It's Always Best
to Pay Your Dues

~

Remnants of ghost towns dot British Columbian road-
sides where, years before, communities once thrived.
These communities were founded around one of the
province's many natural resources, and once those resources
dwindled, or demand for them ceased, industry pulled back
production or shut down altogether. Workers had to look elsewhere in town for employment, and if the demand for jobs outweighed their availability, as was often the case, families were
force to move.

Take, for example, the three communities of Michel,
Natal and Middletown. Tucked away in the southeastern corner
of the province along Highway 3, not far from the town of Spar-
wood, the trio of communities was established near the coal
mines that, in their heyday, provided jobs for hundreds of
mineworkers.

Michel was the first of the three locations to flourish after the Crow's Nest Pass Coal Company opened its mine in 1899. By 1907, the town boasted a population of 1200 residents along with all the amenities any growing community would need. There were a variety of stores, a hotel and even a three-story, 19-bed hospital—a necessity given the dangers involved in coal mining. Workplace accidents weren't uncommon, and some miners lost their lives in the pits. And yet it isn't the ghost of one of these unfortunate workers that haunted this town or, more particularly, the Michel Hotel. The ghost that established itself in the hotel in the 1930s and refused to leave until the structure, which was one of the town's last remaining buildings, was levelled in 2010 had a far more sinister origin.

The Michel Hotel was built of cast concrete in the late 1920s and served as a place where miners and their families could get together and socialize. It was erected during Michel's heyday and was meant to act as a community centre of sorts. Although it fulfilled its role as an important part of the community, the hotel didn't prosper to the same extent as the local mines had. Part of the problem was that the single miners who rented rooms instead of finding permanent, more expensive accommodations frequently skipped out on paying their bills. They simply left the hotel one day and didn't return.

This was a particularly troublesome problem during the Great Depression era. In fact, it was such a common occurrence that the hotel's owner decided to take matters into his own hands. He was done with losing money and decided to take drastic measures. No one was going to skip out on his or her bill again and live to tell the tale.

This is where a young fellow known only as George comes into the story. George thought he'd slip away unnoticed without settling his tab. It is not known if George had done that kind of thing before, or if he even owed more than a day's stay, but one thing was certain—he would never skip out on a bill again. When George left the Michel Hotel without paying, the hotel's owner pledged to hunt down the delinquent customer and make an example of him. And when he finally found George, that's exactly what he did. He dragged him back to the hotel under great protest from George who, by then, was ready to hand over the cash. Unfortunately for him, that didn't satisfy the owner. It's unclear if the hotelier fashioned a makeshift gallows on the hotel's front porch, or if he just picked a sturdy tree at some other public location in Michel. Regardless, he strung George up and left him to die.

The public hanging had the desired effect of deterring other would-be skippers. However, it was George, and not the hotel owner, who had the last laugh in this battle of wills. George's spirit was soon seen wandering the halls on the third floor of the Michel Hotel, or sitting in a vacant chair near the room he'd stayed in before his death. Visitors to the hotel also reported that their candles or flashlights would flicker or extinguish when passing that room, and some claimed his spirit would obstruct their way and prevent them from going down the hall. These reports makes one wonder whether the hotel owner accomplished anything by making an example of George other than scaring off customers.

George's ghost isn't the only one that's believed to have haunted the Michel Hotel before it was demolished on May 30, 2010. The spirit of a woman who committed suicide while staying in one of the rooms has been blamed for the strange sound of running water on the third floor. What makes the phenomenon particularly unsettling is that there is no plumbing on that floor; therefore, no reasonable explanation for the sound can be given.

Chapter 16

The Ghost of Ambrose Small

~

Lights, camera—ACTION! When it came to the high life of the entertainment industry, theatre magnate Ambrose Small loved it all: the glamour, the excitement, the money and the women! To be fair, one might suggest that life in the fast lane was really the only life Ambrose had ever known. His father owned Toronto's Warden Hotel, a modest but successful business, and from the age of 13 Ambrose worked by his father's side. One of his responsibilities was to book shows and musical acts for the hotel bar. That, coupled with another part-time job Small had as an usher at the Grand Opera House, cemented his growing love for show business.

By the time he was a young man, his most earnest desire was to eventually have the financial means necessary to purchase the Grand Opera House. He worked his way up to the position of booking manager and had a flair for acquiring what many thought were more risqué acts than good taste should allow. Regardless the criticism some might have levelled his way in a city that, at the time, was nicknamed the "Methodist Rome," Small's decisions brought in the crowds, and he was making a name for himself. He was also amassing enough money to purchase several other small theatres in the Toronto area. But it took many more years of persistence before Small was finally able to convince the owners of the Grand Opera House to sell.

Despite his victory buy, Small's favourite theatre purchase was undoubtedly London's Grand Theatre. Small is credited with building the theatre, which is also known as the New Grand Opera House. From its opening night on September 9, 1901, it has offered patrons the best in entertainment from every era. But its history is shrouded in a century-long mystery that has captivated anyone who hears of it more than any theatre event held there—and it all has to do with its founder, the mysterious Ambrose Small himself.

Ambrose Small wasn't just known for his finesse at running a theatre. By the time he secured his growing enterprise, he'd become known as somewhat of a rogue. He loved to gamble, was particularly fond of horse racing, and wasn't beyond fixing a race in his favour. He also enjoyed the ladies, especially the flamboyant personalities of the kind of showgirls he routinely hired.

Perhaps it was in an effort to save what was left of his tattered reputation that Small married Theresa. To outward appearances, Small and his wife were cut from very different cloth. Theresa was said to be a devout Catholic with a heart for the poor and an inclination to use her money to help those in need; Small was more enamoured with the nightlife and using his money to enhance his personal enjoyment. What might have drawn Small to Theresa was the fact that she came from money, and the way Small spent it, there was never really enough to do everything he wanted. It wasn't long before Small was dipping into his wife's coffers to add to his string of theatres. Given Ambrose's taste in entertainment and his wife's more conservative views, this could only have caused strain in the marriage.

For 17 years the couple managed their affairs together, but to anyone who knew them, it seemed theirs was more a marriage of convenience than one based on love. Ambrose continued to flirt with the ladies, even after he met one Miss Clara Smith, who became a longstanding mistress. Theresa, on the other hand, busied herself with charitable works.

As they say, all good things must come to an end. By 1919, Ambrose was starting to tire of theatre life. Despite himself, he was beginning to slow down, and by December he had a buyer for his small chain of theatres. Trans-Canada Theatres Limited, a British-owned firm, had offered the Smalls $1 million down, with another $700,000 being paid over five years. It was time, Ambrose believed, to really enjoy the fruits of his labour, maybe even travel a little, and the couple accepted the offer. On December 2, 1919, Small accepted the $1 million down payment. Both Ambrose and Theresa endorsed the check and deposited it into their joint account at the Dominion Bank at 11:45 that morning. From there, the couple had lunch, after which Ambrose returned to the Grand Opera House. Later that same afternoon his attorney joined him for a quick meeting.

It had been an exhausting, albeit profitable day, and the theatre magnate was more than ready to go home. The night was a blustery one. Ambrose pulled up his coat collar and grabbed his scarf as he ventured out into the night. As was his custom, he stopped by a newsstand on the corner of Adelaide and Yonge streets at around 5:30 PM to check out that day's racing results. Unfortunately the train that delivered the papers had been delayed in a snowstorm, and they hadn't arrived. Newsstand owner Ralph Savein said the news left Small in a foul mood. Savein watched as Ambrose pulled his coat even tighter and disappeared into the night, never to be seen again.

Small had been missing for several days before the police were notified. Initially, no one was concerned because he was frequently unaccounted for, thanks to his flamboyant lifestyle. That said, the delay in reporting his absence put Theresa in a questionable light with the authorities. Perhaps it was an effort to stay public criticism, or it was out of genuine concern, but once the investigation was underway Theresa offered a $50,000 reward for information on the whereabouts of her husband. Authorities from several jurisdictions joined forces, conducting what was at that time one of the largest manhunts in Canadian history. But even with the hefty reward money and the assistance of every amateur sleuth with a hankering to get involved in a real case, Ambrose Small was nowhere to be found.

At the same time as police were looking for Ambrose, they were also searching for Small's secretary, John Doughty. Now that he'd sold his theatres, Small no longer had need for a secretary, but he made sure the new owners would keep Doughty on, and with a salary increase at that. Ambrose no doubt expected Doughty to be happy with the arrangements, but Doughty was anything but. Instead, he broke into Small's safety deposit box, stole $100,000 in Victory bonds and took off. It's not clear why he had such an extreme reaction to his change of circumstances, but his actions put him in the spotlight as a possible suspect in Ambrose's disappearance. Was it possible that Doughty had been angry enough to murder his former employer, and if he had, where did he dispose of the body?

The law eventually caught up with Doughty nine months later; he was using the name Charles B. Cooper and was employed at a paper mill in Portland, Oregon. He was arrested for the theft of the bonds, but there was no evidence he had anything to do with Small's disappearance.

Meanwhile, back in Toronto, Theresa was coming up against some public controversy of her own. With Ambrose gone, and presumed dead, several attempts were made to prevent Theresa from inheriting her husband's estate. Rumours circulated suggesting Theresa wasn't the paragon of virtue everyone believed her to be. Some believed she had a lover, and the two had conspired to murder Ambrose and do away with his body. Others believed Theresa was tired of her husband's behaviour. A great number of important people believed Ambrose's choice of entertainers made his theatre chain little better than porn outlets or strip clubs. Because Theresa's money often backed her husband's business decisions, some felt she was as guilty of poor taste as he was. After all, she was profiting from his business decisions. Some people speculated that if she were frustrated with having her name sullied alongside her husband's, it made sense that Theresa would put an end to her husband's scandalous behaviour.

However, it was clear that Ambrose and his wife sold the theatre chain on the very day Ambrose disappeared, so it was unlikely that Theresa had organized her husband's disappearance for theatre-related reasons. But there was still the matter of a possible lover, and because of these suspicions, the basement of the Small mansion was torn up. Other leads focused the authorities' attention on the grounds surrounding the Small home, and they too were excavated. In addition, businesses were searched, the Toronto Bay dredged, and parts of the Grand Opera House were dismantled, all in hopes of locating the man's body. Even the furnace at the Grand Opera House was sifted through just in case whoever was responsible for Ambrose's murder decided to burn the evidence.

As other witnesses came forward with stories of sightings, police widened the scope of their investigation. One report described Small being stuffed into the back seat of a car while other informants claimed they'd spotted the man living it up in Mexico, South America and even France. According to a report in the *Sarnia Observer*, dated Thursday, December 15, 1960, "Toronto police chased 22,000 miles following up clues [and] thirty-five men dug up a Toronto dump" in search of Ambrose Small. None of the leads amounted to a single piece of hard evidence.

At one point in the investigation, which remained active until the file was permanently closed in 1960, there was talk that Sir Arthur Conan Doyle himself would be called in to consult on the case. That request was never made official. However, Vienna criminologist Dr. Maximilian Langsner was contacted. An exorbitant amount of money was spent putting Langsner up in a first-class Toronto hotel, where he claimed to use his psychic abilities to conduct séances and astral trips in an effort to connect with Ambrose. Langsner's "leads" kept police busy for quite some time before they pulled the plug on the man's costly services.

It took Small's wife 15 years in court to finally clear her name so she could collect her husband's estate. Unfortunately, her involvement in her husband's disappearance wouldn't escape future consideration. A letter penned by the lead investigator of the case and discovered in 2001 reportedly suggested Theresa "not only arranged her husband's murder, but was present when it took place," and claimed that officials covered up the entire affair. There is no indication given as to why that would have been the case. The theory is also in direct opposition to another theory that suggests Theresa had been interrogated so ruthlessly because she was Catholic and had promised to donate her husband's estate to the Catholic Church. Toronto at the time was a very Protestant city, and because Ambrose was Methodist, many believed his estate should be donated to causes supporting the Methodist Church.

Ambrose was officially declared dead in 1923, and even though there was little room for doubt that the man had been murdered, a few naysayers believed Ambrose had simply run off and started a new life in some exotic location. Although the official files on the case were closed in 1960, any tips that trickle

in and look promising continue to be followed up by the Toronto
Police. Five years after closing the file on the Ambrose Small
case Toronto police were called to the Rosedale Valley to exam-
ine a possible gravesite. Unfortunately, nothing came of the
matter.

The story of Ambrose Small continues to tantalize the
public's imagination, perhaps because he still makes an appearance from time to time. Stories of his ghost appearing at the
Grand Theatre before a performance or visiting entertainers in
backstage dressing rooms began circulating long before official
investigations ceased. Over the years performers have come forward saying they'd seen his ghostly visage near a stairway or
walking the stage, and since the late 1940s performers and theatre officials alike have reported seeing the spirit of Ambrose
Small walk the stage of his favourite theatre on opening nights.
To this day, workers at the Grand have reported feeling strange
sensations and have seen auras, especially when working at the
facility after hours.

Such stories notwithstanding, almost a century has
passed since the man disappeared into a wintry Toronto night,
and not a single clue as to his fate has ever surfaced. Does his
visage continue to reach out in the hope that someone will
finally uncover what happened to him? Or is it possible that his
ghost still wants to enjoy the nightlife and isn't ready to move
on? We may never know the answer to those questions, but one
thing is certain. If the events of the past several decades are any
indication, the spirit of Ambrose Small isn't about to slip into
oblivion any time soon.

Chapter 17

Lemon's Diggings

~

Commonly considered one of the most valuable and sought-after minerals ever discovered, gold has caused the rise and fall of many a man and nation. Gold was used as currency in the Old World as far back as 700 BC, but it wasn't until 1828 that the precious metal was discovered in North America. Over the next several decades, the discovery of gold in BC and the Yukon paved the way for money-hungry miners to traverse our vast country in the hopes of laying a claim. Every one of those prospectors was an eccentric in their own right; it seemed to be a prerequisite for the job. Yet amid such a wide assortment of temperament, personality and disposition, two characters of dubious distinction stood out among the rest.

It was the spring of 1870 when fate connected two miners most commonly known as Lemon and Blackjack. Lemon is described as about 5 feet, 10 inches in height with a stocky build. He may have been a blacksmith prior to the onset of his mining career, when he made his way from Cedar Creek, Montana, to BC and eventually Alberta. Sources vary as to his first name, but most who knew him referred to him simply as Lemon.

While Lemon was a newcomer to the field of gold exploration, Blackjack was hailed by many in the industry as the best prospector in the west and the man who really discovered the Cariboo diggings in BC. Blackjack, whose given name may have been Nehemiah, had jumped on the gold bandwagon during the Fraser River Gold Rush of 1858. It made sense for a man of brawn like Lemon to connect with a colleague with such vast experience and success, and the two had their eyes set on exploring the lesser trodden lands of southern Alberta. Financially backed by Pennsylvania-born Lafayette French, the two traversed a large expanse of land that took them from Tobacco Plains, Montana, along old First Nations' pack trails through what was at the time considered hostile Blackfoot territory, to High River, Alberta, and then back to Tobacco Plains. As they travelled, the men stopped to dig explorative pits in specific locations along the way.

One evening after a particularly long day of digging, as Lemon and Blackjack packed their gear onto their Cayuse horses and were making their way back in from the picket line, they happened upon the ledge that the gold they had been finding in the area came from. It wasn't just a vein with small gold deposits, but a solid, wide vein with little rock in it.

Unbridled excitement over their find, and the intense greed it produced, sent sparks flying between Lemon and

Blackjack. It was an unbelievable strike and immediately the two men began arguing about what they should do next. They couldn't decide if they should set up camp and stake their find right away, or if they should keep their discovery quiet for a while and return in the spring. It was getting late, so the first order of business was to set up camp for the night. They could take the evening to think their situation through and hopefully come to an agreement in the morning.

Exhausted, both men crawled into their respective bed-rolls. Blackjack fell asleep almost immediately, but Lemon wasn't ready to retire just yet. Instead, Lemon carefully emerged from his bed and started pacing. He was unable to control the anxiety building inside him and didn't for a moment trust Blackjack to share the wealth of their find.

Without giving himself a chance to think his decision through, Lemon crept across the camp to the fire pit where the axe they'd used to chop firewood lay. Grasping its handle firmly, Lemon rushed back to the spot where Blackjack lay and slammed the axe down into his head. Not an especially violent man by nature, Lemon was said to have been paralyzed with horror by what he had just done. As Blackjack's blood pooled around his lifeless body, staining the earth beneath it, Lemon snapped. He began pacing the campsite again, stepping faster and faster, until his heart throbbed so hard he was sure it would leap from his chest. The woods that, earlier in the day, had seemed so serene now felt sinister and suffocating. In an effort to stave off the darkness, Lemon hurled more and more logs on the fire until tongues of flame reached so high they threatened to consume the surrounding forest. Every so often Lemon swore he could hear Blackjack moaning, but the sounds came from scattered directions. Was it possible, Lemon wondered, that Blackjack's spirit was already on the move and plotting revenge?

Come morning, Lemon readied himself to return to Tobacco Plains. Without the benefit of a night's sleep, he had sense enough to remove the nuggets and placer deposits Blackjack was carrying from the previous few days, but he didn't seem to consider the benefits of burying Blackjack's body. He did, however, have a plan. He would visit his old friend, Father Jean L'Heureaux. Lemon believed the priest would protect him and would know how to handle the authorities.

While Lemon's discovery might have sounded like a wild and embellished story, the gold nugget he showed at its telling served as considerable proof of its validity. When he spoke with L'Heureaux, Lemon admitted to killing Blackjack, but the priest was concerned about keeping that part of the miner's story confidential for more than clerical reasons. L'Heureaux had a reputation for being a man of questionable character, especially when it came to following the rules and expectations of his office. In fact, it may very well have been the case that L'Heureaux wasn't a priest at all, but a charlatan and a fraud who was more interested in finding gold and acquiring the wealth that came with it than he ever was in serving God.

The first order of business was to clean up the crime scene. L'Heureaux managed this by sending a Métis tracker named John McDougall to the area to deal with Blackjack's remains. Using Lemon's directions as a guide, McDougall had no problem locating the site and disposing of Blackjack's body as requested. Meanwhile, Lemon was still an emotional wreck, and L'Heureaux spent the winter caring for him; he needed Lemon to remember where that vein of gold was located.

By spring Lemon wasn't much improved, but L'Heureaux pushed on with his plan to have Lemon guide them all back to the site. McDougall had located it without any trouble months before, so L'Heureaux didn't anticipate there'd be any difficulty finding it this time around. He couldn't have been more wrong. Lemon's mental state had deteriorated to such an extent that he basically led them in circles, and the vein, which had come to be known as "Lemon's Diggings," was no where to be found.

When it was obvious Lemon couldn't locate the spot, L'Heureaux called on McDougall to lead another team. It made sense that because he'd been able to locate Blackjack's body without any difficulty, McDougall should be able to find the site again with equal ease. Unfortunately, McDougall was out of town when he received L'Heureaux's request, and although he agreed to lead the expedition on his return, it was not to be. After a night of indulging in rotgut whisky, a potent mixture of wine, water, hard alcohol, chewing tobacco, red peppers, Jamaican ginger, black molasses and assorted other ingredients, McDougall died.

Over the following two years L'Heureaux attempted several times to locate Lemon's Diggings, but each attempt was met with disaster. In time Lemon's mental state had deteriorated to such an extent that L'Heureaux arranged for the man to move to his brother's ranch in Texas. Eventually, L'Heureaux admitted defeat. Finding Lemon's Diggings was not to be—at least not in L'Heureaux's lifetime. Lafayette French, the man who bankrolled Lemon and Blackjack's original expedition, also made repeated attempts to discover the elusive strike. He too met with failure. It was as if the spirit of the murdered miner guarded the strike, preventing anyone, especially his one-time partner and murderer, from ever sharing in its claim.

There was another theory as to why no one could locate Lemon's Diggings. Legend has it that two brothers from a local Stoney tribe were lurking in the woods when Lemon murdered Blackjack. They not only witnessed the murder, they hung around until Lemon left and checked out the site. They too noticed the glistening vein, and returned to their village to tell Chief Jacob Bearspaw their story. Concerned that a gold strike would bring with it an influx of prospectors to the area and, as a result, destroy their people's hunting grounds, the chief forbade the brothers from telling anyone else what they'd witnessed. Some suggest that he placed a curse on the area to prevent anyone from finding the mine.

There may be some truth to the curse because according to the legend of the long lost Lemon mine, bad luck would befall anyone who attempted to locate it. This belief was proven time and time again as fortune hunters who shrugged off the warning met with horrible deaths or misfortune. The leader of one expedition died suddenly of unknown causes, though rumours suggest he drank himself to death while searching for the mine. Another died from horrific burns he'd suffered when his cabin caught fire. Others have since lost every penny of their life savings trying to locate the gold.

Is it the curse placed by Chief Jacob Bearspaw that protects this golden secret? Or does the spirit of Blackjack continue to haunt the woods and greedily protect the claim that would have, in this life, made him a mighty rich man?

Chapter 18
Murdered Hotelier Stays On

~

The murder of British Columbian hotelier Walter Herzog made front-page headlines in 1973. Twenty-three-year-old Norman Morris Stevens of Ganges, Saltspring Island, was charged with unloading five bullets into Herzog's chest and stomach after Stevens burned through the door of the suite Herzog kept at Harbour House, the hotel he owned and managed on the island. Robbery seemed to be the motive behind the attack; the money Herzog was known to have had in his possession was missing. It was a brutal crime for a relatively small payout.

The Harbour House hotel was a labour of love for Herzog. The Port Coquitlam man purchased the building two years earlier and had been commuting back and forth to Saltspring Island as he constructed a new wing, complete with a beer parlour, cocktail lounge and additional guest accommodation. His construction plans expanded when the main body of the hotel burned in the fall of 1972. The night he was attacked, Herzog was planning an official grand reopening. He'd put everything he had into making his project sparkle and shine. Now that all his renovations were complete, Herzog was going to hire a formal manager and enjoy the fruits of his labour. He certainly would not have imagined his life could be in danger.

Perhaps because Herzog was brutally and senselessly shot down, many believe his spirit hasn't left the hotel he so loved. It's his ghost that visitors have reported seeing roam the building and its surrounding gardens, checking up on things and, on occasion, pranking the current owners.

Employees and residents alike frequently claim to hear someone moaning and whispering throughout the property. Electrical appliances in the hotel have acted up, starting or stopping on their own. Then there's the sound of someone sweeping the floors or moving furniture when no one is present. Or the fact that the jukebox gets mysteriously unplugged on a fairly regular basis, and extended games of pinball occur when no one can be seen playing the game.

Much of the paranormal activity occurs in suite 206, which is directly above the site where Herzog was murdered. It was a suite often provided to entertainers spending a few days performing at the hotel. But because of the many strange and unexplained incidents that occurred, band members would often forgo a comfortable bed in the hotel in favour of sleeping in their van; it seemed as though there were times when Herzog's ghost wasn't happy with the manager's choice of musicians.

And then there was the problem of phone calls coming from that same room, even when it was vacant. Try as they might, management couldn't figure out why the calls kept coming in, and they were never able to prove that someone was pulling a prank. In an attempt to rectify the situation, the phone lines were disconnected to Room 206. Even that didn't stop the switchboard from lighting up with calls apparently originating from the room.

Not every visitor to the establishment shared the same experience though. Authors Jo-Anne Christensen and Barbara Smith spent a night at the hotel in suite 206, hoping to partake in an otherworldly experience; it would certainly have added a personal touch to Smith's book, *Ghost Stories and Mysterious Creatures of British Columbia*. Unfortunately, the pair "slept undisturbed in the room where the phantom's frolics have sent many a macho young man screaming into the night."

Does Walter's ghost choose to remain at the hotel he so loved? Or is his spirit trapped and in need of being set free?

Chapter 19

The Root of All Evil

~

If you saw a photograph of George Stanley Kavanagh, you'd most likely agree that he looked like a simple, unassuming fellow. Although a February 9, 1906, article in the *St. John Daily Sun* described him as having "the face of a very bad character," he was slight in stature, with hands that "denote from their softness and smallness and delicacy that he has not been engaged in manual occupation."

It's unclear if the man wasn't able to do manual labour or simply wasn't so inclined. But a look into his past, with time served in a Dublin prison for robbery, suggests he preferred to make his money the easiest and quickest way possible. And with pure greed as a motivator, Kavanagh contrived what at the time was billed as "one of the most brutal crimes ever committed" in Nova Scotia's history.

According to an account published by the West Hants Historical Society, Kavanagh's story begins in late January 1906, when he arrived in the small community of Ellershouse,

Nova Scotia, and took up residence with 66-year-old Freeman Harvie. On the night of Friday, February 2, Harvie was busy working on the local school's taxes when Joseph Fisher and his son, David, stopped by for a visit. While the three men were talking, Kavanagh came in the back door but didn't join in the conversation. Instead, he disappeared into his room.

The Fishers left around 8:00 PM, and soon after, Kavanagh committed his butchery. Armed with a small but recently sharpened knife that he reportedly borrowed from David Fisher, Kavanagh came up behind Harvie and slit the man's throat. He then brought in a saw and decapitated the man. Afterward, he hauled the corpse down to the basement and hid it under a pile of potatoes.

Prior to Harvie's murder, Kavanagh had been announcing his intention to purchase some property in the area. The day after the murder, Kavanagh visited the Fisher home and said he'd succeeded in that quest, and had actually managed to talk Harvie into selling his property. Kavanagh even had the deed to prove it. The Fishers were surprised. Harvie hadn't given any indication he planned on selling when they were talking with him just hours before. When it seemed like they might want to discuss the sale with Harvie, Kavanagh told them he had already left town to finalize the deal with his lawyer.

In the meantime, Kavanagh was going to use the day to settle more permanently into his new digs. Being the neighbourly sort of people the Fishers were, they, along with another neighbour named Edgar McCarthy, offered to help. Kavanagh took them up on their offer but told them to stay out of the porch area and basement. No reason was given for this off-limits designation, which certainly left everyone curious, but they respected Kavanagh's request. After all, it was now his house. To thank them for their help, Kavanagh had the Fishers and McCarthy stay for supper. This inevitably entailed going downstairs to gather some potatoes for the meal and making sure no one followed him.

By Sunday, Kavanagh was becoming increasingly paranoid that someone would go into the basement when he wasn't there to prevent that from happening, so he decided to nail the basement door shut. This, of course, only fuelled the Fishers' curiosity. When Kavanagh began to hastily sell anything of value that was in the house, the residents of Ellershouse became uniformly suspicious. Kavanagh must have suspected as much because he was apprehended near the railway tracks on his way out of town shortly after McCarthy and Joseph Fisher broke open the basement door and found Harvie's decapitated body.

It was determined that aside from the murderer, Joseph and his son were the last to see Harvie alive. In fact, no one knew of the man's whereabouts until his decapitated body was found in the cellar; the missing head was later found in a corner of the cellar in an overturned bucket. Because he was one of the last known people to see Harvie alive, Joseph Fisher was arrested for assisting Kavanagh in Harvie's murder. Edgar McCarthy was also arrested. After all, McCarthy and Fisher had discovered the body and, according to Kavanagh, they were the ones responsible for the murder in the first place. However, the charges against the two men were later dropped when the court decided the evidence supported the claim that Kavanagh acted alone.

In spite of the fact that Kavanagh had just moved into the area shortly before Harvie's murder, several witnesses came forward with stories about him. One woman, a former landlady, went so far as to describe a conversation she had with Kavanagh when serving him breakfast one day. She said he'd murdered an old man in Ireland after being "forced" to do it by a secret society known as the Whitecaps. That bit of circumstantial evidence didn't seem to merit further investigation, but it wasn't necessary for convincing the jury of Kavanagh's guilt. His own actions were all the proof they needed. On February 8, the jury delivered a guilty verdict in the case against Kavanagh. According to the *St. John Daily Sun*, Kavanagh seemed genuinely surprised and reportedly told one of the jurors that he "should not expect intelligent gentlemen like you to sit and listen to a pack of lies."

Before his date with the hangman's noose on August 1, 1906, Kavanagh wrote no fewer than 15 letters to newspapers, both in Canada and Ireland, and to politicians and even friends, looking for financial support to fight his case further. Kavanagh claimed his letters were written "in the interests of justice and humanity." They not only proclaimed his innocence, they described his outrage at the claims written against him in the press. Strangely, none of the letters were ever mailed; they, along with the noose used to hang Kavanagh, can still be found in the West Hants Historical Society's Museum in Windsor.

While Kavanagh was obviously unsettled about his conviction, it's not his ghost that is believed to haunt Ellershouse and neighbouring Windsor. It's Freeman Harvie's headless apparition that Judge Charles Edgar DeWolfe reported seeing in a basement window some years later. DeWolfe was familiar with the story of the beheading and was convinced that the spectre he saw was none other than Freeman Harvie. After his first sighting, other things started happening—strange occurrences that weren't limited by time and space. For example, when the judge was walking home one day, an empty barrel came rolling down the street and stopped on the judge's lawn just as he arrived. From inside the barrel DeWolfe heard a voice moaning out the words, "I am Freeman Harvie."

Also, when the judge walked into certain stores, furniture would move around the room or chairs would start to rock. Light bulbs would smash to the ground for no apparent reason. He saw old coins fall from overhead and items, like an apple, hurl themselves across a room. The occurrences were so frequent that DeWolfe was beginning to wonder if Harvie's ghost had honed in on him for some reason. Was it possible that Harvie's spirit was following him throughout Windsor, or were others exposed to its shenanigans, too? DeWolfe went so far as to question other residents about their experiences, and he logged their statements. Convinced Harvie's spirit was active throughout town and to many people, DeWolfe decided to contact renowned British investigator Hereward Carrington of the American Psychical Institute and Laboratory in New York for his help in the matter.

Carrington arrived in Windsor ready to work. DeWolfe toured the man around all the locations where DeWolfe had experienced unexplained occurrences. And although DeWolfe was convinced that Harvie's spirit was responsible for all that he had experienced, Carrington had his doubts. With a keen detective's eye he watched the body language of the people he interviewed, examined furniture to see if anyone had tampered with anything, and outright challenged some of the stories he was hearing. His final report wasn't what DeWolfe was expecting: Carrington believed that everything DeWolfe had experienced was the result of an elaborate, community-wide practical joke.

DeWolfe found it impossible to believe that an entire town could be in on a practical joke. Even with proof that chairs had been rigged to move when DeWolfe entered a store, and regardless of Carrington's report, DeWolfe believed that Harvie's spirit was reaching out from beyond the grave, trying to make sense of his senseless death. Carrington might have effectively explained away many of the strange phenomena DeWolfe had experienced, but not even Carrington could prove that someone hoaxed DeWolfe way back when he first saw Harvie's headless ghost through the basement window. As far as DeWolfe was concerned, he knew what he saw.

To this day the story of Headless Harvie is known among the residents and visitors of Hants County. And there are some, like DeWolfe, who believe the man's spirit still roams about, looking to make sense of it all.

Chapter 20
Gibraltar Point Lighthouse

~

The city of Toronto is home to no less than 36 National Historic Sites and 50 buildings listed as historic places, but one of its most intriguing and oldest structures has yet to make it on either of those prestigious lists. This edifice has, however, earned the distinction of being home to the city's most enduring ghost story.

According to the historic plaque erected at this particular location, Lieutenant Governor Simcoe chose York (now Toronto) to become Upper Canada's naval and military centre because it had a large harbour that would be easy to defend. Gibraltar Point juts out slightly from that part of the shoreline of Lake Ontario and was therefore the most likely location on which to erect at least one of the lighthouses that would be required to safely guide ships to port.

Historic documents record that in March 1803, an act was passed stating that a lighthouse was "essential to the safety of vessels, boats, rafts and other craft" in two specific locations, one being Gibraltar Point. However, it wasn't until March 9, 1808, that the *Upper Canada Gazette* reported construction of that lighthouse would soon begin, and on April 6 of the same year the exact site was chosen.

Construction commenced, with stone being transported from Queenston, near Niagara Falls. By 1809, the building was operational. The walls, measuring 1.8 metres thick at the base of the hexagon-shaped tower, initially measured 15.8 metres in height. The lantern secured at the top of the lighthouse was lit by hundreds of gallons of whale oil each year. Years later another 9 metres was added to the building's height. That addition, coupled with a revolving electronic light, meant the safety beacon could reach even farther into Lake Ontario than was originally possible.

For almost 150 years the lighthouse guided ships into the harbour under the direction of 10 different lighthouse keepers. But it was the first lighthouse keeper, John Paul Rademuller, who left the biggest mark on the historic building.

Rademuller was born in Anspach, Bavaria, in 1763 and didn't arrive in Canada until 1804. Initially he'd hoped to build himself a little homestead on some Crown land. When that didn't work out, he taught English to German-speaking children for a few years before being appointed as the first keeper of the Gibraltar Point Lighthouse in 1809. He married Magdalene Burkholder a year later, and the couple had a daughter named Arabella. By all accounts the man was known as a good-natured character.

According to some renditions of the tale, Rademuller was also an entrepreneur of sorts. He happily tended his lighthouse duties for six years while allegedly having a small but profitable sideline brewing and selling bootlegged ale. Soldiers stationed at the blockhouse on Gibraltar Point would often hike down the sandbar to the lighthouse and share a drink or two with the amiable fellow. But there were times when Rademuller had to call it a night before his companions were ready to do so, and that wasn't always met with an agreeable attitude.

It was just that kind of scenario that proved to be deadly for Rademuller. Details are sketchy, but it seems that on the night of January 2, 1815, two soldiers with the Glengarry Light Infantry, John Blueman and John Henry, paid the keeper a visit. Whether it was because they didn't have the resources to pay for their drinks or because he thought they'd had as many as they could handle, Rademuller decided to call it a night. His guests, however, were not of the same mind, and a dispute erupted between the lighthouse keeper and two soldiers.

Some renditions of the story describe how the man was brutally beaten and stabbed to death with a bayonet. His body was chopped into bits and buried all around the grounds in an effort to cover up the crime. Surely such a brutal murder would have caused a lot of noise, alerting Rademuller's wife and child, and created a bloody mess that would have been difficult to clean up, but details surrounding the crime scene aren't forthcoming.

It is known, thanks to extensive research conducted by author Eamonn O'Keeffe, that Blueman and Henry were indicted for Rademuller's murder on March 31. And while oral tradition suggests Rademuller's body was never discovered, if that were the case it would have been documented in the news stories of the day. In the December 2015 issue of *The Fife and Drum*, O'Keeffe points out that historic accounts don't mention anything about the man's wife and daughter. Perhaps they were visiting relatives at another location, as surely, if they were present, Magdalene would have testified to what happened in court. Records from the trial proceedings are lost to history, but it is known that the men were acquitted of Rademuller's murder on April 15, and no one else was ever charged for the crime.

William Halloway didn't take over the helm at the lighthouse until the year after Rademuller disappeared. In 1853, George Durnan became the fourth lighthouse keeper, a position he took over from his father, James, and maintained until 1908. In 1893, Durnan was digging in the sand on the property near the keeper's cabin when his shovel hit wood. Curious, he continued to dig until he uncovered what he believed to be the remnants of a wooden casket about a metre under the surface. He also discovered a human jawbone nearby.

There were no records of a death at the lighthouse except for the story of Rademuller, so even without the advances in DNA technology we have today, it seems logical to suggest that the remains uncovered were his. Many versions of the legend suggest his murderers hastily buried Rademuller, but if that was the case they surely wouldn't have had a coffin handy to bury him in. It's more likely the man's body was discovered and later buried near the home he loved.

Of course the discovery of bones believed to belong to Rademuller isn't the climax of this story. Many believe the man never really left his lighthouse home, and his spirit continues to wander the grounds late at night or linger at the top of the lighthouse watching for ships coming into the harbour. More ghoulish accounts bring his murder into the equation, describing the sound of someone running up the lighthouse steps as if trying to get away from an attacker. Others have reported seeing blood bubbling from the 13th step, where some think the murder took place.

On October 30, 2009, around the time of year when most publications are looking for a suitably macabre story to add to their pages to get readers into the spirit of Halloween, *Torontoist* reporter Jacqueline Martinz spoke to parks employee Joe Padovani. Padovani shared an incident he'd experienced back in the early 1980s. It was spring and Padovani was working alongside another handyman named Lionel fixing some stair runners that needed attention. At one point Padovani "looked around and saw that at the base [of the stairs] was an opening to a long, cylindrical shaft." According to Padovani, they "went down, and Lionel and I rummaged around. We found a candlestick holder and then I found the bone that goes from the knee to the hip." He immediately called his superintendent and was instructed to leave everything untouched so the police could check it out the next day. But when the police arrived, the bone was gone. Was it possible someone was playing a prank, or had

Rademuller's ghost cleaned up the site before anyone else saw the bones?

In 1999, Manuel Cappel took on the task of voluntarily manning the lighthouse. He told writer Dennis Smith it was a labour of love, but one that came with a few unsettling moments. "She's aesthetically and architecturally beautiful. During the day she's serene and welcoming. But at night, she can be downright creepy."

If the above stories don't convince you that the Gibraltar Point Lighthouse is haunted, the plaque mounted directly on the building should remove any lingering doubt. The last line on that plaque reads: "The mysterious disappearance of its first keeper, J. P. Rademuller, in 1815 and the subsequent discovery nearby of part of a human skeleton enhanced its reputation as a haunted building."

Chapter 21

Murder of a Gentleman

~

Mail Online, a member of DMG Media, formerly Associated Newspapers, ran an interesting article back in December 2012. The story highlighted the results of a survey that asked modern women which era in history produced the most desirable men. The majority—61 percent, in fact—chose the men of the 1950s as the best catches.

The reasons were simple. The men in the 1950s knew how to be gentlemen. They had good grooming and had more important things to worry about than keeping up their fake tan. They had manners; they knew that something as simple as opening a door for a lady was a sign of respect. These gents knew how to communicate, exuded confidence and weren't afraid to intervene for a cause. And despite the fact that this survey was already a few years old at the time of this writing, a quick Google search on the subject of what women desire most in a man today comes up with most of those same criteria.

In many ways, 44-year-old Richard (Dick) Butler was exactly the kind of man that women would label a gentleman. As the publisher of the weekly *Jasper Place Citizen*, and a local councillor, Butler was a man with his finger on the pulse of the community. He kept up with the issues of the day, lobbied for change where it was needed and worked tirelessly to make his community a better place for his wife and five children, and everyone else under his charge. Butler was also a deputy fire chief and was always ready to jump in and help when needed, even if that meant putting his own safety in jeopardy.

One August morning in 1958, Butler was called to do exactly that. Sixty-five-year-old James Alix lived near the corner of 112th Avenue and 150th Street in what is today Edmonton but at that time was the hamlet of West Jasper Place; the area wasn't amalgamated into Edmonton until 1964. Alix was a reclusive man who, neighbours would have uniformly agreed, was admittedly eccentric. Today's tiny house movement aside, how many people would opt to live in an old boxcar on their property, fortified with a home-dug moat? According to neighbours, Alix had lived there for 12 years and had been digging trenches around his home and throughout his property since he'd arrived. And yet, as unconventional as he was, Alix seemed to be harmless and usually kept pretty much to himself. But everything changed on that hot August day; that day the senior went from oddball eccentric to a dangerous and deadly man.

Most of the reports of the event don't suggest an impetus for Alix's break from reality, but a 2012 story from the *Edmonton Journal* did suggest that storm sewer lines being installed along the street might have been what pushed him over the edge. Whether he thought the upgrade would infringe on his property or affect his taxes, or whether he just didn't like the idea of strangers hanging around his home, Alix was agitated. Equipped with a firearm, he wended his way though his trenches, scoped out the neighbourhood for a time and then opened fire. The shots hit a car parked across the street and embedded themselves into a house located across from Alix's makeshift home.

Initially two constables, whose identities aren't mentioned in the various reports I've come across, were dispatched to the scene. They tried to calm the man and reason with him, but none of their efforts met with the desired success. When it became clear Alix would not be placated, they called for backup. Reinforcements came in the form of additional police, as well as a fire truck.

It's not clear how Butler became involved in the armed standoff. Some have suggested he was at the scene right from the start because it was his home across from Alix's boxcar that was on the receiving end of the madman's gunfire. Others place Butler at the scene without explanation. Regardless whether Butler lived in the area or not, as deputy fire chief he would have eventually made it there with the fire department, especially given the gravity of the situation. Back in 1958 there were only two murders a year for the area that is now the city of Edmonton, so a madman shooting up the streets in an armed standoff would not only have been big news, it would have brought out a good many first responders of Butler's standing.

When reasoning with Alix failed, other techniques were employed. Fire hoses pumped water into the boxcar to hopefully flush the man out. Unfortunately, that only resulted in Jasper Place Chief Barney Weygood getting wounded while Alix was still barricaded in his home and firing shots. Butler suggested using tear gas grenades because they could act as a diversion and, perhaps, smoke him out. That too failed.

Although everyone's patience was being sorely tested, diplomacy prevailed. But a crowd of onlookers had gathered, and when one of Alix's bullets narrowly missed hitting a mother pushing a baby carriage, Butler decided to push the envelope. He'd had enough; something had to be done before the hail of bullets ricocheting in all directions hit an innocent bystander.

Armed with a police revolver, Butler did something that would probably never be allowed to happen today. He sashayed around the fire trucks and police cars and tried to get nearer to Alix's boxcar. He no doubt took the revolver for self-defence, or perhaps to injure Alix enough that one of the officers would be able to contain him. Unfortunately, the one shot Butler managed to squeeze off didn't hit its intended target. Instead, Alix opened fire again, and two shotgun pellets hit Butler in the chest, killing him instantly.

It was a tragic scenario, made even sadder because of the senselessness of it all. It took a bulldozer barging onto Alix's property to drive him out of his boxcar. He was charged with Butler's murder but was declared insane and therefore not responsible for his actions. Alix was committed to the Oliver Mental Institute, now known as the Alberta Hospital Edmonton, putting an end to what was, at that time, one of the most frightening situations in the area's history.

Butler's earthly body had passed on, but his sacrifice had made him a hero to the residents of West Jasper Place. His memory was honoured with the establishment of Butler Memorial Park, located at Stony Plain Road and 157 Street.

The park remains a testament to one man's courageous heart, but much of the surrounding landscape has changed considerably since 1958. Neighbourhoods grew, especially following the amalgamation with Edmonton, and with the growing population came the addition of amenities that every community needs. Shops, grocers, gas stations, laundromats and, of course, an assortment of restaurants all sprang up in the area. And it was in one of those restaurants, a simple hamburger joint built near the location of that deadly gun battle, where Butler's spirit is believed to reside.

Throughout the years, many staff members and even some patrons have agreed there's an odd aura about the place, especially in the staff area. It generally *feels* haunted, but it's also more than a feeling. Items such as pencils and shoes have been known to randomly move position or location, or even disappear altogether. These kinds of things happened with such frequency, and to so many random items, that staff members began to take notice. They were sure it wasn't just a matter of misplacing things or a prank.

By far the strangest meandering item was the moving high chair. No matter where it was put away in the restaurant, it would just roll itself to another location. This moving high chair is also the reason why people who know of Butler's story believe it's his ghost that's responsible. They believe it's possible that Butler's spirit continues to watch out for the safety of children who find their way into an area that was once the scene of such danger and violence.

Chapter 22

Working for Both Sides?

~

A quaint two-story Georgian structure called Auberge Willow by the Lake looks out over Québec's Lac Des Deux Montagnes (Lake of Two Mountains), near the village of Hudson. A short 45-minutes from the heart of Montréal, the building now offers a welcome retreat for travellers and weary city dwellers alike. But when it was erected in 1820, the building was a private residence for George Mallette and his family. François Xavier Desjardins purchased it in 1824. Desjardins operated a store out of the building and, given the fact that he was gathering and storing firearms and ammunition "for the Cause" in his cellar, many believe it doubled as a place where Patriote insurgents met during the Rebellion of 1837, plotting their attack strategy for the uprising of Saint-Eustache.

While the rebels went about their affairs, a servant girl named Maude catered to their more immediate needs like preparing and serving meals, clearing their tables or bringing them something to drink. But unbeknownst to anyone at the residence, Maude was more than just a servant girl. Details don't explain her background or why she in effect operated as a spy for the militia, but as she was attending to her responsibilities, she was also listening intently to the conversation at hand. After gathering whatever information she could, she reported back to an unknown contact.

Her efforts must have proved to be of some value because within four days of the start of the Rebellion, the Patriotes were defeated in the Battle of Saint-Eustache. Maude, however, paid the ultimate penalty for her loyalties. When the Patriotes learned she was a traitor to them she was brutally murdered, and her body was allegedly buried in the basement of the home.

Over the years the building transformed from a private residence to a boarding house, then to a residential hotel and finally into a combination pub/dining room and inn called the Auberge Willow by the Lake. Comments from patrons uniformly praise the accommodations, as well as the food, friendly service and amazing setting. But visitors and employees alike have also commented on another kind of experience they've shared at the inn—a paranormal experience.

Objects moving randomly and without the aid of a human hand, or chairs crashing to the floor when no one is around are common themes in these stories. Some guests have reported hearing the sound of furniture moving or noise in the common hallway, only to find no one else is around. The feeling of being watched or of a presence in the room are other commonalities, as are reports of cold spots. People also report feeling a cold draft as though someone has brushed past them.

Perhaps the strangest story was aired in 2002 by a Canadian television documentary series dedicated to paranormal activity. Some of the staff on site at the time explained to the crew that the most frightening place in the building was the basement. The story goes that "mushrooms grown down in the cellar area, above the spot where Maude is thought to be buried, are found 'beheaded.' Employees have also reported finding piles of rocks outside the door of Room 8, of hearing someone singing pretty songs when there is no one near or smelling perfume waft by even though no one else is present."

Some establishments seem to enjoy boasting about the spirits that wander their halls; however, based on the information provided on its website, The Auberge Willow seems to prefer to be silent on the matter. It is interesting to note, though, that the inn is mentioned on the Haunted Places Canada website. And at least one former owner went on record as saying he didn't know what to make of the claims.

"All I go on is what I've picked up in the 20 years since I've owned the inn," explained one-time owner, Michael Dobbie. "I'll be frank with you. There have been so many stories and a lot of intermingling between fact and fiction. Over the years I've heard so much that I have a hard time deciphering the truth myself."

While history can back the claim that the house was used as a meeting place, as evidenced by the fact that Desjardins found himself imprisoned and facing charges of treason following the Battle of St. Eustache, proof of the existence and death of the young servant girl is scarce at best.

In 1989, the original building burned to the ground. The inn was rebuilt with every effort to maintain its historical integrity. Some paranormal enthusiasts believe the event might have released Maude's imprisoned spirit while others, including some employees who've worked in the new building, have at times sensed a strange atmosphere.

Since the new building was erected, employees have noticed that strange disturbances seem to begin around Halloween and last for about a month. That said, not everyone who's ever worked at the inn has shared in these experiences. One front desk receptionist who worked there for 13 years said she'd never noticed anything ghostly about her workplace. "I grew up in Hudson, and I remember the old inn and hearing stories about Maude, but I can't say I've been affected by her."

Chapter 23

Just Doing Her Job

~

Marvels of architecture sometimes survive the ages even if they've been abandoned and sit as empty relics taking up real estate and providing no monetary return. Such is the case of the Canada Permanent Building, also known as Century House, located on Richards Street in Vancouver, BC. It was constructed between January 1, 1911, and January 1, 1912, and according to its description on the Canadian Register is recognized as a "fine example of sophisticated Beaux-Arts style architecture, featuring interior and exterior materials and craftsmanship of a highly refined quality." Also according to the Canadian Register, the building was constructed to "convey a sense of permanence, conservatism and security," and on September 23, 1986, it was formally recognized as an official Canadian Historic Place.

The building has housed a number of occupants since its first tenants, the Canada Permanent Mortgage Corporation, closed their doors in 1951. One of the most recent businesses to operate at that location was a restaurant called the Century House. Of course morphing into a restaurant required extensive remodeling, and it was during this time that workers reported several strange sightings. The general consensus among the workers was that there was at least one ghost inhabiting the building, and it was a woman. Unaware of earlier rumours that the building might be haunted, a carpenter working on the remodel reportedly noticed a strangely clad woman wandering the construction site. Irritated by her presence, and concerned for her safety, he asked the woman to leave. The glare in her eyes as she turned to face him had the carpenter fleeing instead.

The end of construction might have brought with it fine cuisine and a faux-Tuscan atmosphere, but it didn't spell the end to the paranormal sightings. Even more disturbing were the mournful sobs that seemed to come from one of the stalls in the ladies' washroom. According to an account detailed in the blog Ghosts of Vancouver, when another woman in the ladies' room checked in the stall, it was empty and the crying ceased.

Over the years an explanation has been offered for the origin of the sad ghost who cries in the bathroom and frightens off construction workers. Legend has it that during the building's first incarnation as a bank, a robbery occurred. Unfortunately, the money stolen wasn't the bank's biggest loss; a young, defenceless female teller was shot to death.

Another version of the legend suggests the woman's death was at the hand of her own husband. The man, angry at some perceived slight, confronted his wife at work and shot her in the presence of her coworkers. She died instantly. In both renditions of the story, it's this innocent victim who's said to haunt the building to this day.

While the story of the murdered bank teller has been widely circulated, it's important to note the sources haven't backed the claim with news articles or police reports on the robbery. That said, so many people have experienced what they believe is a paranormal experience at that site that it's clear something untoward happened there.

The Century House restaurant closed its doors in 2011. As of the writing of this book, the building at 432 Richards Street remains empty except, perhaps, for the wandering spirit of a woman wronged.

Chapter 24

A Call from the Grave?

~

Alfred Cecil Pearce was a typical family man living with his wife and three daughters. He worked hard for a living, as most folks do, and in 1948 he and his wife became the proud owners of their very own home in Calgary. True, the small cottage located at 1805 20 Avenue N.W. was an older home; built a few decades before the Pearces purchased it, the home had seen at least 20 years worth of short-term tenants who either neglected or outright mistreated it. Still, the building and the property it sat on sold for a great price. It had great potential, and the Pearces were anxious to get started on making it feel more inviting.

Their daughters weren't too pleased with their parents' plans for the weekend they moved in. It was the beginning of July when the family made their move from Port Alberni, British Columbia, and that was Calgary Stampede weekend. Surely their parents didn't expect them to forgo the event and wait an entire, long year before experiencing the glam and colour of a rodeo of such size and caliber? The very least their parents could do was take them to the big event. Mom and Dad did not agree. There was a lot of work to be done just to make the house livable, and that was by far a priority over attending a rodeo.

If asked, the girls would have told their parents that nothing would make that house feel homey. There was something downright creepy about the place, especially in the back bedroom where each of the girls said they'd felt a cold hand grabbing at their ankles. When they told their parents what they'd experienced, their concerns were bushed aside as a poor excuse to get out of work.

At the same time, Alfred had noticed a squeaking sound and a "springy" feeling from some of the floorboards in that particular bedroom, and while he was in the fixing mood he thought he should check it out. Since there was no visible reason why the floors should squeak, Alfred reasoned the cause of the problem was beneath the boards. It pained him to think of the job at hand. While much of the house needed a lot of TLC, the floors in this room were expertly done. There was no way he had the skill to replace the floorboards after he discovered the problem. Despite his dismay, with saw and crowbar in hand, Alfred jarred loose one plank; he never pulled up a second.

Alfred may have not known what to expect, but he would probably have bet his life savings it wouldn't be what he found. Dropping his tools on the floor, Alfred rushed from the room to the front door, bumping into his wife along the way.

He told her to stay out of the back room and keep the girls away; he needed to find a telephone and call the police. Alfred's behaviour stunned his family. Never before had he acted so frantically and because of that, all four women stayed away from that room and huddled together by the front door until Alfred returned.

Officers Gordon Gilkes and Frank Whiteside were dispatched from the closest Calgary detachment. Police work is always full of surprises, but a call like the one they'd just received from Mr. Pearce definitely fell under the one-of-a-kind category. At the same time, the man had just moved, and was likely under a lot of stress. Perhaps he was overtired or confused, or maybe a former owner had buried a favourite dog on the property and no one knew it was there until Alfred started pulling the floorboards. The entire scenario could simply be the result of a comical misunderstanding. Then again, Mr. Pearce might have very well found a corpse buried underneath his home. If that was the case, there was no doubt they had a murder on their hands.

When police arrived at the scene, Alfred escorted them to the back bedroom. Sure enough, only one floorboard had been removed, but it was enough for the officers to know they indeed had a body on their hands. They also had a mountain of work before them, starting with pulling up the rest of the floorboards to expose the entirety of what was, in effect, a grave.

Finding a body underneath a person's house would be disconcerting to most, but aside from the gruesome discovery, investigators reported feeling uncomfortable while in the house.

As the Pearce girls would have said, the place was creepy. To take their minds off the disturbing sensation they turned on the radio, only to have it turn off on its own accord, or dial in between stations and produce only static, leaving the men even more unsettled.

Before long, most of the beautifully crafted floor had been pulled up, revealing a very calculated gravesite underneath. According to the Calgary Police Service Interpretive Centre and Archives, a photograph of the site "reveals that the murderer sawed out a section of the floor joists to create the 'grave' [and that] the feet had been barely six inches from the edge of the house."

In her book, *Deadly Encounters: True Crime Stories of Alberta*, author Barbara Smith shares Officer Gilkes' findings. He described how a body was "partially exposed lying in a shallow grave of ashes" and how it had "apparently absorbed all the moisture and sort of mummified." Gilkes went on to describe the size and shape of the body, the clothes and even the small ring that still clung to what remained of a baby finger. Gilkes also noted a "large jagged hole" in what they presumed by size to be a man's left temple, along with another smaller hole behind the man's ear. An envelope was also discovered near the body, addressed to a Mr. Thomas C. Hall at the aforementioned address, and sent by one Wallace Hall of High River. The postmark was dated 1929.

The first order of business was to track down Thomas' wife, Camilla, and their three sons, John, Fred and Charles. John, a decorated war vet and pilot, was the youngest of Hall's children. When called on to identify the remains, John said he couldn't positively identify the body as belonging to his father. His brother Fred, on the other hand, shared no such doubt, nor did Thomas' brother, Wallace.

Wallace was equally shocked and relieved when police were dispatched to his High River home with the news that they thought they'd located his brother. Wallace told the police that he was relieved to finally know what became of his brother, as it had been so long since he'd disappeared.

The police requested that Wallace visit his brother's former home and view what they believed were Thomas' remains, and so the man made the trip into Calgary. When Gilkes met Wallace at the front door of the Pearce's home, the officer was reportedly stunned. Even after 20 years of decomposition the family resemblance between the brothers made it undeniable; the body in the basement could be none other than the missing Thomas. "The fellow came to the door and just from looking at the body which was mummified [and the man at the door], I knew it was his brother," Smith reported. There was also the matter of the "celluloid ring inscribed 99." According to the Hall boys, the ring was known as a "chicken ring" and was a symbol of the poultry business Thomas once owned, removing any doubt as to the body's identity.

Following the positive identification, a post mortem examination was conducted. It was determined that someone exerted considerable force, striking Thomas in the head several times and cracking his skull, causing his death. A full-fledged investigation unearthed a lot of theories, but even more questions. Why would someone kill Thomas Hall? And what of the logistics of burying the body under the floorboards of a rental house? Surely the rental agency responsible for the property would have checked the building over the years. Was there no smell from the body following its burial? And what about the floors? Who could have so expertly redone the floors?

A closer look at the man's family life raised even more questions. Thomas may have swept his young wife, Camilla, off her feet and produced three strapping young lads with her, but they were far from a happy family. At some point during their tenancy, Thomas and Camilla had separated, leaving Thomas and his youngest son, John, living alone in that house. By all accounts, Thomas was a mean and bitter man who was at the very least, verbally abusive to his children. Fred and Charles, the two oldest boys, had been living on their own for some time. When Camilla moved out and set up her own accommodations in the city, 15-year-old John was the only one at home to catch the brunt of the old man's wrath.

Then suddenly, in March of 1929, Thomas disappeared. It seems no one reported the man missing. In truth, it seems no one actually acknowledged his absence at all, which is strange given the fact that he was responsible for paying the rent and providing for a minor who was still in his care. It wasn't until June that the Crown Trust Corporation, the rental agency managing the property, decided to investigate. The Halls had been longstanding tenants who paid their rent like clockwork, so when more than two months had passed and rent hadn't been

paid, it was time to see what was going on. When a representa-
tive from the company came to check it out, they found the
home deserted and unlocked, but clean and well kept. A cursory
check didn't uncover Thomas Hall's whereabouts, and because
it was quite possible that he simply moved on with one of his
many business ventures, and it was clear the family had moved
out, the Crown Trust Corporation got on with the job of finding new tenants. It seemed to be an ongoing job from that time
on as no tenant lived in the house for more than a few months;
there was just an eerie feel about the place. That constant turno-
ver was another reason why the Pearce family was able to buy
the house at such a bargain price.

No one was ever charged with the man's murder, though
the Calgary Police Service Interpretive Centre and Archives
does note that the authorities at the time of the investigation
believed that they knew who was responsible for the murder, but
could not lay charges against their suspect. No clear motive for
the murder was ever determined, either. Hall did have some
money, but he had no will and no insurance, so money doesn't
seem to have been the motive.

Why didn't Thomas' brother, his estranged wife, or even
his sons report him missing? Was he such a tyrant that everyone
was so relieved by his absence they didn't want to find him?
How can a man be murdered and buried in his own home and
no one associated with the individual suspect anything untoward had occurred? And who secured the efforts of a master
craftsman to rebuild the floors in the back bedroom without
anyone noticing Thomas' shallow grave in the process?

The murder of Thomas C. Hall remains an unsolved case. While Thomas's body finally received a proper burial on Monday, July 26, 1948, that didn't put a rest to the strange happenings in and around the home. Doing a little investigation of their own, the Pearce family discovered that previous owners also felt an unexplainable and unreasonable unease around the house. Barbara Smith reported that a man named Rick Passey owned the house much later, in 1982. Passey also admitted to feeling an eerie presence in the home, and there were many times when he heard a knocking at the front door but when he checked, no one was there.

Is the ghost of Thomas C. Hall still calling out for justice? Or is it possible that the man who was reportedly so unkind in life has simply continued on, spreading bad karma in death?

Chapter 25

A Spectre Roams this Place

~

Anyone who's travelled through New Brunswick will agree that it's a province with lush green forest. Even today, more than 85 percent of the province is forested, and that forest is strictly managed. Forty-eight percent of the province is designated Crown land, 30 percent is privately owned and 22 percent is designated freehold. But as early as the mid-19th century, more than 80 percent of the province's exports were made up of forest products; clearly the province managed this renewable resource well.

Lumber camps attracted strong men from as far away as across the Atlantic. At about the same time, between the years 1845 and 1852, Ireland was struggling through the infamous Great Famine as a blight ravaged the mainstay of their economy, the potato crop. More than 1 million peopled died of starvation and disease. Entire families were wiped out. And many families boarded so called "coffin ships" and headed west, hoping they might be able to establish a better life for themselves in the New World.

That was what led the gentleman of this story to a lumber camp along the Dungarvon River, a tributary of the Renous River in Central New Brunswick. As with most tales that date back more than 100 years, details are sketchy. Take the name of this story's main character, for example. The identity of the tall, dark and handsome Irish man with a strong physique and curly hair is vague at best, but in most renditions of the tale he's referred to only as Ryan. Whether he came directly from Ireland to the cooking job he landed at the aforementioned lumber camp, or if he lived elsewhere first isn't known. But when Ryan arrived at his new job, his personality immediately won over his workmates. He was a character, waking up the boys with whoops and hollers. His unwelcome exuberance might have jarred them from their sleep, but Ryan served up a mighty fine breakfast so no one really minded.

Ryan was also a terribly trusting individual. He didn't seem to understand that some things one should keep to oneself, and so there really wasn't a lot of mystery to the fellow. He arrived at the logging camp with all his worldly possessions, which, he was quick to inform his camp mates, included his entire bankroll. He kept the money safely wrapped around his waist in his money belt, which wasn't strange given the time in Canada's history when this story takes place and the lack of easily accessible banks anywhere nearby. However, he carelessly flaunted his stash, which included coins and large bills that added up to a sum that would raise more than a few eyebrows. He was no doubt cautioned to keep his personal finances to himself, but Ryan didn't worry. He liked the guys and he trusted them.

One day a new boss appeared at camp and overheard talk about Ryan's loaded money belt. The men headed out to the site, but the boss announced he planned to stay behind. It was odd that on his first day on the job their boss would opt to send his men to the logging site alone while he stayed back at the camp. Surely he needed to assess what they were doing for himself, rather than relying on reports from the previous boss? Strange though it seemed, the man was their boss and the men dutifully left for their day's work.

Later that evening the loggers noticed that the familiar aromas that Ryan had treated them to weren't wafting in the breeze to greet them as they returned from their long day. Supper wasn't on the table—and it wasn't being prepared either. In fact, the suppers they'd come to look forward to wouldn't be tempting their taste buds any longer. Their cook was dead, his lifeless body crumbled on the mess tent floor. Their new boss suggested that Ryan had fallen and hit his head after experiencing some kind of convulsion, but camp workers had quite another idea about what happened. Ryan's money belt was still around his waist, but it was open—and it was empty. The loss of personal property certainly wouldn't have been the result of a fall.

It was clear the man had been murdered, but surprisingly no one dared to push their boss on the matter. Neither did anyone challenge the man about what might have happened to the missing money from Ryan's money belt. Someone must have thought about the fact that although he was dead, he might have had a family he was providing for. Surely it was their duty to find his family and send that money on. However, if anyone thought the situation merited an investigation, no one—not a single soul—spoke up on Ryan's behalf.

A wicked storm was brewing, so preparations were hastily made to inter Ryan's body in the forest. The young man's corpse was laid in a shallow grave, and the men bowed their heads for a moment or two of respectful silence before covering it over and heading back to camp. Life certainly wouldn't be the same without Ryan's rousing wake-up call every morning.

Silently the men walked on, each mulling over the situation in their own way. Suddenly they stopped dead in their tracks. The wind had picked up, whipping tree branches in every direction and kicking up much of the forest floor in the process. But it wasn't the wind and it's ghastly moaning, nor was it the torrential rain that froze the men in their tracks. It was the ungodly shrieking and wailing of a man in pain that terrified their hearts. It was Ryan's voice, they were certain. But it wasn't the jovial man they knew who called out from beyond the grave. It was a tortured soul calling for recompense. Horrified, the men stumbled back to camp hoping that, come morning, the storm would have passed and with it the dreadful wailing.

That wasn't the case. In the middle of the afternoon, as the sun fell, as the moon hovered overhead, no matter the time of day, screams and hollers would suddenly echo through the woods, sounding like a man gone mad. According to the legend, the sounds drove the men crazy with fear, and before long anyone who knew Ryan fled the camp for good; they felt partially responsible for what happened to him given the fact they didn't push for answers on his behalf.

That said, their absence didn't stop the ghostly sounds. Other lumberjacks who'd come up to work the site were equally troubled by the bone-chilling sounds that seemed to come out of nowhere. Because Ryan's story was well known in the logging community, someone eventually came up with the idea of calling in a priest from neighbouring Renous to help put the poor man's spirit to rest. Father Murdock presided over the case, making his way to the site of the former lumber camp and the general area where it was thought Ryan's body had been buried. The good Father made the sign of the cross and opened his Bible, read from several comforting passages and prayed over the man's soul, guiding it to a sure and perfect rest.

Father Murdock's efforts met with mixed reviews. Many of the men working in the woods and families living nearby have agreed that the ghostly cries have been silenced, and a sense of calm has replaced the previous negative energy. But the story of the murdered Irishman was so ingrained in New Brunswick's history that in 1912 Michael Whelan immortalized the story with his poem, *The Dungarvon Whooper*. It bears mentioning, however, that not everyone agrees with the popular ending to this story. In Whelan's tale, the restless spirit finds peace and is laid to rest. Some, however, argue that the cries of a man whose soul continues to be tortured can still be heard on a stormy New Brunswick night.

Chapter 26

Island Mystery

~

A thin ledge of rock juts out of Lake Superior just south of the tip of Sibley Peninsula, Ontario. At best, the ledge is simply a sliver of rock measuring a mere 25 metres across. And yet at one time, judging by an old and pixelated monochrome image, no less than seven structures once housed a crew of workers on that patch of rock surrounded by unpredictable waters.

It was those unpredictable waters, and the fact that although humans have created many marvels we have yet to be able to tame the mighty waves, that spelled the end to the dream of a mining empire. Thomas Macfarlane first staked a silver claim in the area back in 1868. The Silver Islet Mining Company, headed by one A.H. Sibley, purchased that claim in 1870, and William Bell Frue took over the helm as mine captain. Frue established the buildings on the rock that housed workers, machines and supplies. He organized the building of the crib work necessary to hold back the waters, hauled in loads of crushed rock to secure the false walls that enlarged the island to almost ten times its original size at one point, and managed the mine's overall operations.

It was an endless battle that cost time and money, but considering all its setbacks the mine yielded a considerable haul during its 16 years in operation. About $3.25 million worth of silver was pulled from that mine, with the promise of more to come. Unfortunately, a load of coal required to fuel the pumps working to beat back the lake mysteriously went missing. Without the necessary fuel, the pumps quit working, and most of the 384 metres worth of mine shafts were flooded, spelling the end of an era. At the time it was believed that most of the highest quality silver had been extracted, and rebuilding the mine would cost more money than it was worth.

But there were rumours floating about the site; rumours that suggested a cache of silver was within reach if only someone was brave enough to go after it. Moreover, a reclusive man named James Cawdor believed he'd been instructed as to the whereabouts of these silver nuggets by the voice of a dead miner, and he made no secret of his claim. In fact, he told anyone who'd listen that he'd conversed with this miner's ghost and been given exact instructions on how to retrieve the loot. All he needed was about 30 metres of rope or a sturdy ladder that he could use to lower himself down a particular shaft. If all went well, by nightfall the next day he'd be a wealthy man, Cawdor bragged.

The next day Cawdor headed out as planned, but he didn't return home that night. Concerned neighbours set out to look for him, but there was no sign of what became of the man.

Searchers did not find the rope or ladder he would have needed to pursue his original intent to lower himself into a mineshaft, but Cawdor had been so insistent about his quest that residents were worried about his welfare. A week passed before his bloated and disfigured body was spotted floating in the slimy waters surrounding Silver Islet. His body had to be fished out with a grappling hook. A coroner was brought in from nearby Port Arthur and, despite the many questions surrounding the case, ruled Cawdor's death accidental.

The coroner's ruling aside, there was talk in town that Cawdor had shared his information with the wrong person. That person had followed him to the site and pushed him to his death, disposing of any evidence that Cawdor had scaled the mineshaft and making off with the rumoured silver nuggets. However, rumours don't make a court case and there was no evidence to warrant an investigation and arrest. Cawdor's body was buried and his home boarded up.

Years later, on June 25, 1914, Cawdor's stepdaughter, Leona, had the occasion to meet with the renowned Sir Arthur Conan Doyle. Bill MacDonald chronicled the story in the magazine *Geist*; Cawdor's stepdaughter was MacDonald's aunt. She had always been suspicious about her stepfather's death and wanted one last chance to speak with him and, with any luck, find out once and for all what happened that fated day. Knowing the mystery writer was interested in the spiritual world, Leona attended a talk Doyle was delivering at Port Arthur's Colonial Theatre. After the talk, Leona approached Doyle and shared her stepfather's story. Intrigued, Doyle suggested that a night séance at Cawdor's former home in Silver Islet would be the best way to go. The problem was that he was about to leave Port Arthur and didn't know when he would return. As an interim measure, Doyle and Leona gathered at Cawdor's Port Arthur graveside. Unfortunately, the man's spirit wasn't cooperating, and it seemed like Leona was destined to go to her own grave without the answers she was looking for.

It wasn't until Doyle returned to the area in 1923, almost 10 years later, that Leona got her chance to speak to Cawdor's spirit. Doyle was travelling with his wife, Jean, and again delivering a talk at Port Arthur's Colonial Theatre. As soon as Leona approached him, Doyle remembered her. The two made their way to Silver Islet for that long overdue séance, accompanied Doyle's publicist, Mr. Booth, and his wife Agnes.

This time they congregated at night at Cawdor's abandoned home, and the results were far more productive. The house smelled of mould, and aside from the echo of their footsteps as they made their way across the clapboard floor, the place was ominously silent. Doyle asked Leona, by way of formality, whom it was she wanted to speak with. Her stepfather, she said explaining how he was a good enough fellow with a few shortcomings, not unlike those most of us have. More directly, she described him as a "wishful thinker who sought his fortune in a defunct mine and fell to his death down the open shaft."

Following her description, Doyle conjured up the spirit of the deceased Cawdor. The group heard the sound of muffled footsteps followed by water splashing, and finally the sound of someone letting out a deep sigh. All was silent for a few minutes, then the room filled with the sounds of rattling hinges, jingled chains and other appropriately frightening noises. "Cawdor, is that you?" Doyle reportedly asked. No words were uttered, but Leona felt the slightest touch on her right shoulder, and cold breath against her neck and ears. A dialogue ensued between father and daughter—a dialogue that Doyle witnessed but the daughter did not remember.

Over breakfast the next morning Doyle and his wife, along with the Booths, told Leona what they'd witnessed as the woman and her father communed. The entire experience was at best fuzzy for Leona, but Doyle and his entourage shared how at times the woman's body shook so violently that they were concerned for her safety. Leona, however, seemed satisfied with the results of the previous night and when asked if they should return again, politely declined.

Was James Cawdor the victim of his own over-active imagination? Was his death an accident, as the coroner suggested? Or did someone who overheard his story and was convinced the man was on the trail of something valuable, follow him to the mineshaft and, after the coveted silver nuggets were retrieved, pushed him to his death? Is it possible Leona remembered more of her discussion with her stepfather than she shared with Doyle and his companions? Could Cawdor have told Leona the details surrounding his death, including the identity of the individual who killed him, and for some reason Leona chose to withhold that information?

Today, Silver Islet is listed as one of Ontario's ghost town. There are still a number of homes along the shore being used as summer residences, and the old hotel that once welcomed the likes of Sir Arthur Conan Doyle now serves as a general store. It's a serene location to visit, but don't be surprised if you come up against a ghost or two, especially if you wander the shoreline or venture out in the water near what was once a profitable mine.

Chapter 27

The White Trapper of Labrador

~

Our northeastern-most province of Newfoundland and Labrador is a unique landscape created by some of the oldest rock in the world. Fossils and petrified remains dating back 565 million years have been discovered along the Avalon Peninsula, and the rocks of Gros Morne National Park have earned the area a designation as a United Nations Education Scientific and Cultural Organization (UNESCO) World Heritage Site.

Although the province covers a total area of 405,212 square kilometres, only about 510,000 people live there. Most of those, about 181,000, are nestled in and around St. John's. The remaining residents are scattered in small communities and throughout the countryside; at last count, a scant 28,628 resided in the roughly 295,000 square kilometres that comprise the Labrador portion of the province. If my math is correct, that means if everyone spread, out each person could claim 10 square kilometres of land for themselves.

The relatively small population in this portion of the province means much of Labrador's geography has remained pristine. Newfoundland and Labrador's Department of Tourism calls The Big Land one of the "last untamed, unspoiled places left on earth." It's a land that demands a strong and self-reliant spirit if a person is going to survive. Weather is unpredictable, regardless of the season. Wind speeds of 70 km/h accompanied by whiteout conditions dumping 20 or more centimetres of snow and wind chill temperatures of −45°C or lower aren't uncommon in winter. If you aren't prepared, you could be in a lot of trouble.

Turn back the calendar to the early 1900s and these dangers were even more profound. A trapper might head out on a clear, crisp morning to check his lines and be stuck in a blizzard before the day was done. Get caught on the top of a bald mountain or a barren coastal plain without a means for warmth and protection, and you'd surely fall to the elements.

Esau Dillingham was a Newfoundlander who was up for the challenge. He'd left the island of his birth and moved up to the more rugged landscape of Labrador, hoping to make a good living as a trapper. He was well equipped with his team of 14 dogs and sturdy sled, and he seemed to enjoy being outdoors well enough. What he didn't care for was how much effort he had to put in for such a modest monetary return, all things considered. And so he devised a plan to pad his coffers. He came up with his own recipe for backwoods brew. Mixing sugar, yeast, spruce cones and a few other ingredients, Esau cooked his concoction over an open fire that lent a somewhat smoky taste to the end product. The "smoke," as it became known, might have tasted horrible, but it warmed the gut and numbed the cold and "Smoker," as Esau became known, effectively peddled it to other trappers.

For a time Dillingham was able to keep up with the growing demand for his bootlegged brew and manage his traps; before long, though, the demand for his smoke was so great that he decided to hang up his trapping gear for good and man the kettle full time. Now there's a reason why things like alcohol production are managed by the government. Sure our legislators want a piece of the financial pie, but there's also this little thing called a safety standard. One likes to know the product they're going to ingest isn't going to kill them. Unfortunately for some of Smoker's clientele, that's exactly what happened. Smoker's brew was potent and often poisonous. Some men went mad after consuming the smoke, others went blind, and a few, sadly, died.

Even in a land as barren and unpopulated as Labrador, the local authorities were aware of Smoker, and officers were hot on his tail. Not only was Smoker wanted for his moonshine production, but he took other illegal liberties, as well. Those who knew Smoker described him as a cruel, vicious man who took what he wanted, including women who weren't available for him to take. When other men were out checking their trap lines, Smoker was known to push his way into their homes and rape their wives. In short, he was a brutal man.

While there are variations to the tale, most agree that the authorities eventually caught up with Smoker. He was incarcerated in a St. John's prison for a year, but when he was released he, like so many other criminals, went right back to his previous way of life. There was a difference, though. Smoker had had a year to consider the kinds of improvements he'd make so he wouldn't get caught again when he finally got out of jail. The first thing he did when he returned to Labrador was to paint his sled white, purchase a white fur parka, pants and mittens, and trade in his dog team for 14 all-white huskies. Like the snowshoe hare that blends in to its environment, Smoker would go unnoticed as he passed through a wintery white landscape.

For some time his plan worked. Smoker's clientele continued to grow, despite the fact that many knew they were taking their lives into their own hands by drinking the man's rotgut. And any time officers were narrowing in on their subject, Smoker managed to evade capture.

Smoker likely could have continued his enterprise into his old age had he not done something stupid; he started drinking his own brew. As with much of his clientele, the moonshine didn't make him shine in a good way; it brought out the extremely ugly in an already nasty character. Whatever internal regulators Smoker had before were considerably weakened by his indulgence, and when a customer was being difficult, Smoker would put him in his place without any thought to the consequences.

It seems his temper and poor lifestyle led to his end, although the details of the story differ considerably from one source to another. Some have Smoker dying of natural causes in his cabin, albeit indulging in his smoke could have certainly caused that death. Other versions of his demise are considerably more violent. One story tells of an enraged husband who shot Smoker dead in defence of his wife's honour after Smoker assaulted her. Another story describes him staggering through the wilderness in a drunken haze, falling and breaking his back. But the most popular version has Smoker arrested in 1920 for murdering one of his clients and falling while in jail, breaking his neck.

Although the cause of his death is up for discussion, all sources converge on several points. The man was nasty, and as he was dying he seems to have come to understand the depth of his evil ways. Frightened by the thought of spending all eternity in Hell, Smoker prayed. He asked God's forgiveness and begged for the chance to keep running his dog team in the afterlife, and to use the opportunity to help people in need.

And so it is that the ghost of Esau Dillingham, the Smoker of Labrador, continues to run his dogs along Labrador's cold and wintery landscape, keeping his eyes open for travellers who've lost their way. Many a traveller has told of being trapped by the weather along the desolate Labrador trails and being saved by a man in white, manning an all-white dog sled team. This man usually guides the lost individuals to some kind of safe shelter, only to disappear before they can thank him.

One trapper reported being caught in a blizzard and mushing his dogs against the driving sleet with no sense of where he was going. It wasn't going to end well, he was convinced, but he was going to give it all he had to save his team. That's when he heard the sound of another team echoing in the distance, and getting louder with each mush. Soon he noticed the visage of a man dressed in white fur from head to toe, riding a white sled and leading a team of white dogs. Was it a mirage, he wondered? Was he loosing his grip on reality?

The ghostly image overtook the lost trapper and began to lead the way. For the next 30 minutes it took every ounce of strength the trapper had in him to follow the man to the winter houses of Frenchman's Island. The trapper was overjoyed to see a fisherman open the door and call him inside, but when the trapper turned to thank the man who'd led him to safety, the stranger and his team had disappeared. When the trapper asked the fisherman which way the man in white went, the fisherman denied having seen him.

Almost all of the struggling travellers who were saved by the strange man in white had a similar experience. Often they were the only ones to see the apparition, and there were no tracks left in the snow behind the sled. Once the spirit had guided a traveller to safety, he simply vanished. The most dramatic rescue was perhaps the story of a trapper who'd been checking his traps and got caught in a blizzard. He was alone and far from shelter. Hypothermia was setting in, and he could no longer move when Smoker's ghost appeared. Smoker lifted the man onto his sled, wrapped him in white furs and mushed to the nearest community, where he carried the near-frozen traveller into a hotel and set him in a chair. He nodded to the hotel keeper, instructed him to take care of the man, and faded before the hotelier's very eyes.

Smoker's ghost has also been credited with saving two RCMP officers (which would have more likely been Newfoundland Rangers). The pair had gotten lost while patrolling Labrador's countryside in 1949 after a sudden blizzard caught the officers off guard. They were disoriented and floundering when they noticed a man wrapped in white fur driving a team of white dogs their way. Their best chance at surviving the storm was to follow the musher who seemed to know where he was going. Several hours later they all arrived at an old trapper's cabin. The smoke from the chimney was a welcome sight indeed, and the policemen were overjoyed to see a few other trappers had taken refuge there as well and had a warm fire going. The officers expected the man who'd led them through the blizzard to have followed them inside, but when they turned to thank him, he was gone. On hearing of the officers' experience, the trappers in the cabin were captivated. "It was Smoker," they all agreed, explaining that the officers had been rescued by the ghost of a man who was once a murderer but spends his afterlife trying to do good.

There are countless stories of Smoker's ghost saving lost travellers, but the inconsistencies in these stories leave a lot of questions unanswered. The repeated referral to RCMP could simply be the result of recent retellings by orators who just messed up on their history. But if a man named Esau

Dillingham was indeed arrested for murder, surely there would be an official record of this somewhere. Then again, it's not impossible that official documents could have been destroyed; that kind of thing happens even with today's technology. Perhaps Dillingham's many sins were dealt with in a more local, but no less severe, way. Surely some kind of law enforcement presence made an effort to maintain the peace. Or maybe vigilante justice dealt with the man who believed he was beyond reproach. After all, someone had to keep the peace before official law enforcement came on to the scene.

As with any ghost story, Smoker's tale seems to evolve with each telling. And while the majority of the stories in this collection can be tracked back to some form of official documentation, the story of Smoker is an exception. I opted to include it in this volume because the story is such a vibrant part of Newfoundland and Labrador's oral culture. There are so many reports of the white trapper and his team that I can't believe it doesn't have some basis in fact.

But, as with any other ghost story, we'll probably never know for sure.

Chapter 28

Grande Ghosts

~

When Grande Prairie's York Hotel first opened its doors for business back in 1948, it was considered one of the finest hotels in the north. Peace River Country was beginning to boom with an increase in oil and gas exploration and the development of other natural resources. Towns like Grande Prairie were fighting to become the business centre of northeastern Alberta. A hotel like the York, which was owned and operated by the Logan family for more than 60 years, not only offered travellers a first-rate place to stay, it also offered residents the chance to enjoy a first-class meal in a licensed dining room—a first for Peace Country—and a place to dance. The hotel also housed a number of other businesses over the years, including a law office, a laundry and a taxi stand.

But a lot has changed since 1948. Booms turn bust, and Grande Prairie has had its fair share of economic challenges. By 2010, the hotel was no longer the bustling centre of activity that once drew some of the city's most prestigious citizens.

The structure had begun to deteriorate and the clientele had changed. The once-proud hotel had become a hangout for drug users and street workers.

Dwight Logan, a former mayor of Grande Prairie, spent a good part of his life living and working at that hotel. His family owned and operated the business from the day it was built until it was demolished in 2010. During that time they'd witnessed their fair share of tragedy, starting with the murder of a young female employee. The woman had been working in the basement laundry when her estranged lover hunted her down and shot her dead.

Another death on the premises was recorded as a suicide, but most people who knew the young man believe his death was the result of another murder. In this case, the happy, well-liked man who worked as a bartender and bouncer was found hanging in his bedroom. Logan believed the man got mixed up in the drug world. "We are all sure it wasn't a suicide. There's just no evidence—even the police knew," Logan told reporter Drew Rogers of *theVAULTmagazine*. "He must have crossed them, and this was his payback."

Many locals believe the spirits of these two individuals, who both met a violent end at the York, made the hotel their home. Several employees reported strange activities, and Logan openly recorded them on the hotel's website. According to Logan, an employee he refers to only as Del said she'd clean the lounge area, straightening the tables and chairs, then turn around minutes later to find them askew once again.

Items moving on their own seems to have been commonplace at the York. One employee reported seeing swivel chairs moving by themselves while another witnessed ashtrays sliding across the counter on their own, or even flying through the air. Another employee was alone in the pool room, racking up the billiard balls, but before he could put the rack over them, they all scattered as if they had been pushed.

In her book *Haunted Alberta*, author Barbara Smith describes how another "reported that while working in a storage area and an unused corridor in the basement, he heard the sounds of voices clattering. He was cleaning up the rooms there, and when he went to look, not only was no one there, but also a room that he had cleaned just a few minutes before was trashed. He just cleaned it up again. He also reported being alone in a basement bar area that was quiet at the time when a loud, female voice behind him told him to get out. He turned, and there was no one there." Other employees also heard the sound of people chatting and banging around in that same empty corridor.

Footsteps were reported in other areas of the hotel, as was random whistling or humming, distinct cold spots and even the occasional aura. In one instance an employee referred to by Smith as Cea identified a "very strong cold spot" in the basement. He left but returned some time later to see if the area was still cold. Because there had been considerable open discussion about the hotel being haunted, Cea decided to speak out to what he thought might be an entity, reassuring it that he wasn't going to hurt it. That's when the cold spot changed, becoming even colder.

Electronic devices intermittently went on the fritz in the hotel's cabaret. In particular, a telephone often stopped working for no apparent reason, but when a technician was called in to check it, all was reported to be in proper working order. The same thing happened with the music system in the basement, which malfunctioned on occasion without cause. Cea also reported seeing the needle on a turntable lift up by itself. A dishwasher on the premises frequently started up on its own, and the front desk sometimes received calls from vacant rooms.

Over the years, many employees reported feeling someone touch their shoulders, only to turn and find no one there. In some cases, the spirit of Dwight Logan's brother, Merritt, is believed to be the one reaching out. Merritt, the barroom manager, was a happy and popular fellow. Unfortunately, he too died in his hotel bedroom after succumbing to alcohol poisoning. One employee remembers Merritt touching her shoulder in a certain way, and she believes that he continues to reach out to her even in death.

Was the presence in the basement the spirit of the murdered laundress? Is the ghost of the bouncer reaching out for justice for a crime no one can prove was committed? Or was the hotel a magnet for unsettled spirits from all around Grande Prairie?

The team from Alberta Paranormal Investigators was invited to spend the night in the hotel prior to its demolition on November 1, 2010. They toured the entire building and set up their equipment in locations where most of the activity had been reported. Although they didn't get to experience any of the reported phenomena firsthand, they were subject to a unique experience. After walking through a particular area several times, one of the researchers noticed a man's chain on the ground. Photographs the researchers had taken previously of the area prove it wasn't there on any of their earlier walk-throughs, and no one on the team claimed it as their own. Could the chain's appearance be the result of a paranormal phenomenon?

Chapter 29

All for a Loaf of Bread

~

Picturesque doesn't begin to describe Lane's Privateer Inn in Liverpool, Nova Scotia. The property had several owners, including Captain Joseph Barss, who many believe was the greatest privateer in Nova Scotia's history. In 1947, Edgar and Helen Lane purchased what was by that time essentially a large and neglected rooming house situated on the Mersey River, named for the river in Liverpool, England. The family operated a number of businesses from the location, including a large furniture store and a beauty salon, and they rented out some of the upstairs apartments. But in 1962 the couple decided to change direction somewhat. They expanded, renovated, added a formal restaurant, coffee shop and banquet room, and set the foundation for the Lane's Privateer Inn. Today, residents and visitors alike enjoy this stately hotel, which has become an important cultural hub in the rural community.

With such a lengthy history, the building is bound to have a ghost or two tucked away in one of its many closets. And while there's no definitive proof that something's amok, enough strange reports have been collected through the years to make the inn one of several locations investigated in 2015, during Liverpool's first East Coast ParaCon. This event is organized by Jay and Marie Yates of Crossed Over Paranormal Society (COPS) and the Queen's County Museum.

Susan Lane is the third generation of Lanes to work in the family business. She certainly isn't the only person who has experienced something paranormal at the inn over the years, but she's noted that most of her experiences have taken place over the Christmas season when the inn is closed. She doesn't believe there's any connection between those experiences and the season itself; she reasons that because the inn is empty and quiet, the sounds are more audible.

Susan's first ghostly experience occurred in 1986. It was Christmas Eve, and she'd just returned from having dinner with her parents. She was alone in the inn, taking advantage of the quiet by catching up on some paperwork, when she heard the muffled sounds of a woman crying.

"The experience was very disturbing, but not frightening," she said, adding that she checked throughout the inn just to be sure she was alone. She could find no cause for the sound, but wherever she ventured in the building it remained constant. "Then, almost as quickly as I heard the sobbing, it stopped and almost immediately I began to hear a woman singing a lullaby. I'm sure it was a lullaby although I couldn't recognize the words. It was soothing and mellow and she kept repeating the song over and over as if she was trying to comfort someone, maybe a young child." The song started and stopped intermittently for about 30 minutes before it quit altogether.

Another one of her personal experiences suggesting a ghost might be lurking about occurred on Christmas Eve, 1989. Once again, Susan had been visiting her parents and was returning home to the inn when she noticed what looked like the "blue flicker of a television in one of the windows on the third floor." That wouldn't have been odd had there been guests staying at the hotel, but the inn had a policy of closing for Christmas. When Susan left the inn that night, it had been empty. Was it possible that someone had broken in? The idea of breaking and entering just to watch television certainly didn't make sense and, being the sensible soul she is, Susan thought that perhaps they'd missed turning off a television when the staff had conducted their room checks.

After letting herself into the inn, Susan immediately went up to the third floor. What she discovered was more than just a single room with a television on. "When I got there, all the doors were open," Susan told author Vernon Oickle during an interview in 2001. "Now normally those doors would all be closed and locked. And I knew they had been closed when we locked up for Christmas. It was unsettling, to be sure, but I still made my way down the hallway to room 134 where I thought the television was on. When I got there, I found that the television was on and the noise was blaring quite loud." Needless to say no one doing a room check would have overlooked a roaring television.

Susan also found the room extremely cold; so cold, in fact, that she could see her breath.

"Not really understanding what was happening, I went in and turned off the TV. As I turned it off, the door to that room slammed shut and then I could hear all the other doors slamming closed one after the other, as if someone was running down the hallway closing them as they went. When I went to open the room's door it was locked."

Sure enough, when she stepped out into the hallway she could see all the other doors had closed. When she went to check them, she found they were all locked.

"I don't know how that could have been. In those days... you had to manually lock those doors. It was impossible for them to lock and unlock themselves. There's just no way."

Rare is the employee who hasn't witnessed the ethereal image of a man in black walking in the inn's front door, or looked up to see a figure standing at the end of the bar only to have it disappear before their eyes. People also report feeling cold spots and seeing objects moving or pictures out of place. Unexplained muffled noises can sometimes be heard, and the smell of floral perfume suddenly wafts through the air, especially in the hotel bar.

Stories about room 134 were also quite common, according to Susan's father Ron. "We've had reports of the doors opening and closing by themselves and of things moving about the room. We've also had guests tell us that they sensed a presence in that room and that the presence seems very distressed and uncomfortable," he told Oickle.

There is no solid theory to explain the male presence sensed at Lane's Privateer Inn; the ghost isn't believed to belong to the good Captain Joseph Barss or any other man known to have lived on the property. But there is a theory behind what might have caused the spirit of a woman to linger so long after her death.

Prior to European settlement, the area was the site of a seasonal camp for the Mi'kmaq peoples. They referred to the spot by two names: *Ogomkigeak* (dry sandy place) or *Ogukegeok* (place of departure). Because it was easily accessible, offered great land and an ample fishing harvest, it also attracted explorers like Samuel de Champlain and Nicolas Denys. Liverpool was founded in 1759 and was incorporated as a town in 1897.

Being geographically close to the United States, Liverpool saw quite a lot of conflict spilling over from the American Revolution, and it was a centre for rumrunners during Prohibition. Suffice it to say, administering law and order during these early days in our country's history was challenging.

Hanging was a common punishment for any number of crimes, allegedly because it saved on the cost of incarceration. You didn't have to murder someone to be executed; you could do something as simple as stealing a loaf of bread. That's exactly what legend has it a woman, whose name is lost to history, did sometime shortly after Liverpool was founded. The woman in question was a single mother at a time when that in itself must have been akin to a death sentence. She and her family were starving and, with no other recourse, she stole a loaf of bread. She was allegedly caught in the act and hung from a hanging tree on the very property where Lane's Privateer Inn is now located. If the story is true, there's little wonder why Susan would have heard what she believed was a woman crying and singing lullabies. Hanging a woman for her desperate attempt to feed her children could surely produce a woeful spirit unable to enter into a peaceful afterlife.

Chapter 30

A Good Time Gone Bad

~

First Nations peoples travelled the route through Barrie, Ontario, and its surrounding area long before Europeans came to Simcoe County. Barrie was first officially settled toward the end of the War of 1812 and was incorporated as a town in 1837. It was a growing hub of activity and required the accommodations and entertainment opportunities of any large centre. By the time Barrie became a city, in 1853, there were already six hotels accommodating the roughly 1400 residents, all located in a neighbourhood known as The Five Points. Businessman James E. Dunlop believed the city could use at least one more such establishment, and he opened the James Dunlop Hotel in 1854. It must have done good business because he opened a second hotel called the Simcoe Hotel on the same property, just south of the Dunlop, in 1856.

As they say, location is everything, and the Simcoe definitely had location on its side. Situated at the eastern end of what was then called Penetanguishene Road, which is now

Highway 93, it was the logical place for the thrice-weekly stagecoach to overnight. The stage brought the Simcoe a lot of business, and the steady stream of patrons kept the hotel's coffers filled.

With no less than six watering holes within a stone's throw of each other all doing crisp business, on most nights there was a lot of activity. More often than not patrons were just having a good time, but there are always those rowdies who sour a situation and, after downing too much liquid courage, are looking for a fight. Often a brawl would break out and the law would need to be called in. In particular, the Simcoe Hotel gained quite a reputation for its boisterous clientele throughout much of the 1860s and 1870s.

During this time a local lady named Elizabeth Meyer was known to visit the establishment with considerable regularity. Not much is known about Elizabeth Meyer, other than the fact that she had a particular fondness for cheap booze. She must have also had an equal partiality to the Simcoe Hotel, as it seems to have been her favourite watering hole.

One can only imagine that, back in the 1870s, a woman frequenting a hotel bar to tie one on was a rarity that no one would encourage; she would not have been looked on with much respect. It was no doubt equally ill advised for that woman, after a night of drinking, to walk home alone in the dark. One cold January evening in 1872, that's exactly what Elizabeth did.

Meyer had been at the Simcoe, enjoying the company of her fellow patrons along with her favourite whisky for many hours before deciding to call it a night. In her drunken stupor it was all she could do to stumble to the door and down the hotel's front steps without colliding with another customer in the process. It was a bitterly cold night—considerably colder than it was when she entered the hotel hours earlier, and she pulled her coat tight around her small figure in an effort to protect herself against the wind and driving snow.

As she walked, she wondered if perhaps the cold had kept people indoors. Although she didn't mind walking alone at night, Meyer was glad the streets were empty. Barrie had attracted quite a few undesirables of late, and the city was gaining a reputation for its unbridled lawlessness. Perhaps she was getting a little too old for such foolery as these late night indulgences, she argued with herself. Tomorrow she'd forget about thinking she should mend her ways, but for now she'd be happy to jump into her warm bed and curl up beside her husband.

Her head felt heavy, causing her to stagger down the dirt street, gaining speed with each step until she found herself up against something she hadn't expected. There, in front of her, was a shadowy figure. She squinted to try and clear her vision. She wasn't sure who it was, or what it wanted, but there was a knot forming in the pit of her belly and she was pretty sure it wasn't from the whisky.

Before she could register the full extent of the danger before her, a debilitating blow snapped her head back. The cry she struggled to release stuck in her throat as another, then another punch landed, knocking her flat on her back. Again and again her attacker struck, merciless in his assault and unrelenting in his rage. It all happened so quick, and the blows were so unwavering in their force, that Meyer didn't even have the chance to raise her hand in a feeble attempt to protect herself.

And then, just as suddenly as it began, it was over. Meyer lay dead in the street not far from the hotel where, a few moments before, she was laughing and downing her last drink.

The poor woman's body was discovered the following morning, her limbs sticking out of the freshly fallen snow, the horror of her last moments mirrored in the frozen expression on her face. A cursory investigation couldn't produce a single witness that saw Meyer walking through the street that night. Indeed, if anyone besides Meyer and her assailant had been on the street, they may not have noticed the brutal beating through the driving snow, and they may not have heard her cries over the wailing wind.

Shocked at the find, those gathered around the body moved Meyer's remains into the hotel, where a coroner conducted an inquest. Remarkably, the coroner decided the woman, having consumed too much alcohol, had simply passed out while walking home and died of exposure.

If one lets their imagination run wild, one can devise any number of reasons for such a ridiculous finding. Even to the untrained eye it was clear Meyer had been the victim of a brutal assault. Look at the countless bruises on her face and body, people argued. Surely it was obvious the woman had been murdered.

Is it possible the coroner knew Meyer had been the victim of a homicide and was covering for the killer? Or was the man's hasty judgment simply a matter of disinterest in a poor, drunken, working class woman who should have known better than to party it up every night and wander home in the dark? Regardless the reason, the coroner filed his documents on the case, Meyer was put to rest and the entire matter was dismissed from the public eye.

Or so everyone thought.

In February 1876, the old Simcoe Hotel was destroyed by fire. Done with the unpleasantness that had surrounded his hotel, Dunlop had no interest in rebuilding. An Irishman named Michael Shanacy, however, was keen on the idea. He purchased the property from Dunlop and rebuilt, opening the new hotel under the name Simcoe House. The new establishment was considerably tamer than its former incarnation had been, and the memory of Meyer's tragic death seemed as far removed as the hotel's rowdy past.

The building has changed hands several times over its 140-year history. Each owner has left his or her own mark on the place, and only time will tell if aspirations for a historic overhaul of the building will garner the energy and funding required for the job. But some would argue that the longest-standing resident of the building is the spirit of Elizabeth Meyer.

Author Andrew Hind had occasion to visit the Simcoe Hotel in the early 2000s and spoke with an employee he referred to as Tiffany about the paranormal experiences she'd had during her time there. He explained that once she'd learned the ropes, and had a handle on her responsibilities, she became less stressed about her job and more interested in her environment. That's when Tiffany started noticing the feeling of being followed, or at the very least, of being watched. At first she brushed off the sensation, but when she began to feel a hand touch her on the shoulder only to turn and find no one within an arm's reach, she began to think there was a spiritual energy lurking about.

One particular experience solidified the idea in her mind.

Tiffany left the hotel after a late shift one night not long after Christmas. It was dark and cold, and Tiffany pulled up the collar of her coat to protect herself from the falling sleet and snow. Leaning forward into the wind, Tiffany once again had that strange feeling of being watched. The sensation unnerved Tiffany more as she walked alone down a dark street than it did in the hotel. With her heart racing, she quickly glanced back over her shoulder. When she turned to look ahead again, she was stunned to see the image of a woman standing in front of her.

"She looked three-dimensional, like a real person, but she was kind of indistinct. I couldn't make out her features. I didn't think much of it at first, but the woman just stood there frozen to the spot and staring right at me. I remember thinking there was something cold about the look on her face," Tiffany told Hind.

It was strange that the woman seemed unaffected by the inclement weather, Tiffany remembered thinking as she glanced away from the woman. When she looked back, the woman, or at least her image, was gone. "Even though I couldn't see her, she was still there. I heard the distinct sound of footsteps crunching through the wet snow to pass by me and head toward the restaurant. I even felt an icy cold chill as the now-invisible woman brushed past me. It was only then that my mind registered that I had seen a ghost."

The ethereal image in the night wasn't the only time Tiffany saw what many believe was the spirit of Elizabeth Meyer. One day Tiffany entered a room to find a woman in a long dress "lying stretched out on the floor" and looking "motionless and deathly pale." The temperature in the room suddenly dropped drastically, "as if someone had opened a freezer." Tiffany went to rush to the woman's side to see if there was something she could do to help, only to watch the shape disappear before her eyes.

When asked, Tiffany found it difficult to describe the woman. "The events only lasted a couple of seconds each time, but I just sense that she's been gone a very long time and is very sad. Her death was tragic. She's middle-aged but pretty, and she wears a heavy shawl. But it's just a sense, maybe something my mind is creating as a way of giving my feelings some context."

Others who've been to the hotel have had similar unexplained experiences. Sudden cold spots or drafts have been noticed throughout the building. A former manager reportedly witnessed what looked like the translucent shape of a woman floating down the hallway, only to have it disappear when he tried to approach it. The man then heard footsteps rushing up behind him. When he turned, there was no one there. The experience left him shaken, but he was so determined to prove what he'd experienced was real that he reviewed the hotel's security footage the next day. He couldn't find any evidence of an intruder; his was the only image that appeared on the tape.

Is it possible that the person responsible for the brutal demise of Elizabeth Meyer was held accountable for his actions when he left his earthly existence? Does the spirit of Elizabeth Meyer continue to walk Barrie's Five Points neighbourhood, looking for a sympathetic person to release her into an eternal rest?

Chapter 31

When Suicide is Murder

~

A buse of any kind is devastating. It's not just about the physical scars one receives, often at the hand of someone who should love and protect them. Such bruises eventually heal; however, the emotional scars, which only deepen over time and with each attack, can be every bit as deadly as a physical attack. It is true that victims of abuse can be in constant danger of being murdered by their abuser. Some abuse victims are lucky enough to rise above their situation and make a life for themselves elsewhere. But there are also those victims who, unable to live with their situation, choose to end their lives instead.

Such was the case for a woman named Cassie Smith.

Cassie lived with her husband, Joseph, and their seven children in Port Saxon, a community in Shelburne Municipal District of Shelburne County, Nova Scotia. The legend surrounding the woman doesn't suggest she was a maltreated woman prior to a significant incident that seems to have set her husband against her. One of their children, Sarah, moved to the United States in 1916 and got involved with a man. Finding herself pregnant, the woman was obviously distraught; having an illegitimate child at that time spelled certain shame to one's family. Unable to work through the pain of her situation, the girl hanged herself.

Joseph was devastated by their loss, and to a large extent he blamed his wife for his daughter's death. Joseph believed that Cassie knew of the pregnancy and kept the information from him. He believed that, had he known about Sarah's situation, he may have been able to reach out to her and assure her she was still loved and wanted. Instead, he never had the chance.

At first his fury toward Cassie took the form of angry looks or the short manner with which he spoke to her. Before long, though, it escalated into verbal abuse and hateful accusations that he heaped on her over and over again. Finally came his fists, which landed with such force that Cassie often wondered how she managed to recover. There would come a time, she believed, that Joseph would throw a punch from which she would not get up.

It's not like Cassie didn't try to get away from her abuser. When it became clear that Joseph's anger was growing and not abating over time, she tried to disappear. Admittedly she didn't make it far. When Joseph discovered her, she was sitting by the river not far from their farm. Joseph grabbed her and dragged her back to their home, berating her with every step. Once there, he tossed Cassie into the house and left.

Cassie was spent. She had no fight left. Once Joseph was far enough out of sight, Cassie crept out of the family's farmhouse and made her way into the barn. She grabbed a rope and climbed to the threshing floor. Working quickly she secured one end to a beam and formed a makeshift noose with the other. Pulling it over her head, she secured it around her neck and jumped.

There's not a lot in the legend about Joseph's reaction to this loss, but much has been shared in the oral folklore of the area about the spirit of the woman who'd struggled through so much. For one thing, a horseless wagon began to appear rolling across the field near the Smith's barn. In 1919, neighbour Ephrian Harris and his companion Raymond Stoddart were driving his wagon across a bridge when they saw another team galloping toward them. Harris and Stoddart worried that they were going to be run down. Just when they began to think that they wouldn't survive the crash, the phantom team disappeared. Others experienced the sounds or sights of a horse and wagon team, too.

The form of a headless woman has also been reported flinging herself over the side of the bridge and into the water beneath. Another lady, this one dressed in white, has been seen coaxing a flock of white geese across the highway and then dissipating into the night sky.

In the barn itself, which of course has changed hands and at point belonged to Irvin Webber, has had its fair share of paranormal activity. One day while working in the hayloft, Irvin heard strange sounds coming from the threshing floor below. He said it sounded like someone was being strangled, but when he checked he couldn't see anyone. The sound, however, continued. Irvin didn't need an explanation, really. He knew the cause of what he'd heard—it was the sound of Cassie Smith hanging herself.

Richard Webber's family owned the neighbouring farm. He remembered an experience from his youth when his mother called him and his siblings to the window. "There," his mother said, pointing into the field. When they looked to where she was pointing, they saw a woman covered in a black shawl, floating through the morning fog. Before long, she disappeared altogether. "There's Cassie Smith if I ever saw her."

Back in the house that once belonged to the Smiths, the sounds of footsteps sometimes echoed overhead even when no one was upstairs. Doors would open and, despite being closed and secured, would pop open again. A lamp tipped over and went crashing to the floor, and other objects moved by themselves. There was also a general feeling of another presence in the building.

One night, after working at a community apple-peeling party where neighbours gathered to peel the apples and hang them to dry for baking, Richard was making his way home when he turned to see that every room in the Smith house had been lit up. At that time it would have meant there was a kerosene lamp in every window, which was certainly not the case. But in the blink of an eye the lights went out, and the house was dark again.

The only constant in life is change, and eventually Irvin Webber and his family moved out. Afterward the house remained vacant, and eventually fire destroyed the property. No one knows what started the blaze, but it is hoped that the woman's spirit was finally freed, knowing the home where she'd been so brutalized is no more.

Chapter 32

All Eternity is a Stage

~

Imagine making your way down the aisle of an empty theatre after a show, sweeping up the debris patrons left only to turn around and find the popcorn container you'd just thrown away back in the aisle. So you pick it up again and toss it in your garbage bag. Just to be sure it's where it's supposed to be, and you aren't losing your mind, you tie up the bag, leave it at the end of the aisle and move on. After making your way through the rest of the theatre, you return to pick up the garbage bag and double-check that aisle once more for good measure. Your heart skips a beat as you notice what looks to be that same popcorn container, plus a few errant kernels of popcorn scattered about. The garbage bag looks exactly the way you remembered leaving it, but when you untie the bag to check its contents, you notice the popcorn container is missing.

Creepy?

Absolutely.

But that's not the creepiest experience you might have were you to work at, or visit, Fort Macleod's Empress Theatre.

The Empress Theatre has been dubbed the oldest functioning theatre in western Canada. Construction on the building began in 1910, and its doors opened for the first show in 1912. It was the fourth theatre to open in the small but growing community, and the only one to stand the test of time. Aside from the occasions when it's been closed for renovations, the theatre has been entertaining residents and visitors alike for more than a century. One might also suggest that a lot of improv goes on in the building. They are special showings, if you will, for a few eyes only; but not every audience is entertained.

Finding garbage, like popcorn containers or candy wrappers, tossed about after a cleaner has been through the area is a regular occurrence according to a number of employees who've worked at the theatre over the years. Work there a few shifts and you almost come to expect it. The creaking sounds that resonate throughout the building are a little harder to get used to, as are the occasional shadowy figures that dart across the stage or behind a doorway, or the lights that flash on and off at will. In fact, there are so many strange occurrences that the Empress has also been dubbed the country's most haunted theatre.

The spirits seemed silent at the beginning of the theatre's history. In 1937 Daniel Boyle purchased the property and devoted the majority of his time and energies into maintaining and operating the 450-seat art deco theatre. His extensive renovations included a 100-seat balcony, and for many years the theatre attracted such class acts as Sammy Davis Jr. and, far more recently, Sarah McLachlan. Boyle was considered the theatre's most successful owner, and his tenacity didn't go unnoticed by the members of his community. Unfortunately, Boyle passed away suddenly in 1963. Running a successful theatre business is always a challenge, and the Empress struggled considerably until 1982, when it was purchased by the Fort Macleod Provincial Historic Area Society.

Initial stories that suggested the Empress Theatre might be haunted began circulating in the early 1960s, some time after Boyle's death. Those stories increased in the 1980s, after the latest round of renovations, suggesting to some that the spirit or spirits inhabiting the premises didn't like anyone to disturb the surroundings.

Robert C. Belyk is a Canadian author who has spent considerable time investigating the paranormal. The Empress Theatre was one of several locations he highlighted in his book, *Spirits of the West: Eerie Encounters from the Prairies to the Pacific*. Among the mysterious experiences he described was that of Jay Russell, a member of the Great West Theatre Company.

According to Belyk's account, Russell was alone in the theatre and exploring the building when he came upon what was called the "swamp cooler room," an area so named because of its musky smell. He noticed pieces of an old organ and wanted a closer look. He propped open the door so he could see, using the light from the boiler room, and went inside.

"I reached into the dark, and it's getting darker and darker, and I have my hand extended out trying to reach this old keyboard or whatever it is," he told Belyk. "And just as I touch it, there's this big laugh behind me. Like someone is pulling the funniest joke in the world on me. It wasn't spooky; it was just this big belly laugh. And all of a sudden, the prop on my door was gone and the door slams shut. And then thump, thump, thump up the stairs. Someone was laughing and running up the stairs."

It certainly wasn't funny for Russell who spent the better part of an hour locked in the dark room before he was able to open the door, which suddenly opened with ease. Russell confirmed with theatre staff that there hadn't been anyone in the building at the time, that he was indeed alone.

Russell's experience was unnerving, but it was nothing compared to the stories of people going down to the washroom and looking in the mirror only to see the face of a strange man staring back at them. Several sources share this story, which seems to have been reported at different times and from different people throughout the years. In each case, when the individual turns to confront the man in the mirror they find no one behind them.

Author Barbara Smith shared more ethereal experiences in her book *More Ghost Stories of Alberta*. An actor named Bruce Watson described feeling "a cold spot at the front of the house." He further described how, during an earlier summer appearance at the theatre, he had "a strange feeling someone was standing over my left shoulder down the back stage staircase. I mean, I really felt like there was someone there."

Diana Segboer was a member of the Empress Theatre Society for a time. She too has experienced situations she could find no explanation for. She's heard footsteps when she was alone in the building, and alarms have gone off for no apparent reason.

One day before the theatre opened for the day, Diana and her coworker Joyce opted to take advantage of the quiet time to finish up some odds and ends. "Joyce was humming a tune," she told Smith. "When she stopped, Ed whistled its ending."

Many people who'd heard the ghostly tales believed the spirit lingering in the Empress belonged to its one-time owner, Dan Boyle. But during her tenure with the theatre, Diana had come to refer to the ghost as Ed. She came to that decision because the male image many have reportedly seen is large and somewhat hairy. Boyle was a smaller man, so while he might be responsible for some of the mysterious activities, he's certainly not behind them all.

Ed, on the other hand, has been described by the theatre's website as a cigar-smoking, whisky-swilling gent who sported a cowboy hat and a country drawl. He not only worked at the Empress as a janitor, he also had a side job mucking stalls at the Macleod Auction House. And the enterprising individual allegedly had at least one more diversion; some sources suggest he was a bootlegger.

If that were indeed the case, it could have been the reason why he was murdered sometime in the 1950s. His body was discovered behind the auction house, but no one was ever charged or convicted of the crime.

Is it possible the ghost of Ed the caretaker, with no intention of moving on to his afterlife any time soon, has chosen to add a little spice to the entertainment at the Empress Theatre? If so, his list of shenanigans continues to grow in leaps and bounds with every passing year.

During rehearsals, a burly man with a cowboy hat has been seen sitting in the balcony. There have been times when he's been blamed for the stage curtains closing or lights going out before their time. Prank calls coming from inside the theatre have also been blamed on Ed. And at least one time he has interacted with guests, allegedly selling two girls tickets for a show; they had arrived late to the theatre and by all rights no one should have been at the ticket booth, but they described Ed perfectly.

Paranormal investigators have reviewed photographs that appeared to show images of orbs or other unexplained lights.

Author Jeff Belanger has also recorded stories of the Empress Theatre in his book *The World's Most Haunted Places*. He too suggests the ghost belongs to Ed.

"A lot of people think it's this guy because he was a bit of an alcoholic, he worked at the auction market, and he was a cigar smoker. It seems to be that often when there's a ghost experience, it's followed by the smell of alcohol, manure or cigar smoke. That's why a lot of people think it's this guy," he said.

Chapter 33

Slain Innocents

~

The city of St. John's, Newfoundland and Labrador, also goes by the moniker "City of Legends," and it does so for good reason. The port has the distinction of being the oldest and most easterly in North America and has seen more than 500 years of rich history. Perhaps it's because of that lengthy history that St. John's is also considered by many to be one of this country's most haunted cities.

As Sue Bailey of *The Canadian Press* once put it, "People here swap tales of haunted houses, supernatural signs, and the deeds of friendly or mischievous spirits as if they're discussing the weather." A paranormal account centred on 92 Queen's Road, in St. John's, is one such legend.

The three-story building was equipped with three apartments, one on each floor. A husband, wife and their children inhabited the top floor while that family's grandmother occupied the second floor. The story goes that the grandmother, who was quite elderly at the time, repeatedly mentioned hearing babies crying. Now her grandchildren were much older, and there were no babies living in the building at the time. Reasoning that she was simply hearing things, the woman's family dismissed her complaints.

But the grandmother wouldn't give up. She insisted she heard babies crying; there were at least two, she was certain. And to add to the frustration, the grandmother was sure she'd seen a mysterious woman slowly making her way up to the third floor apartment on several occasions.

Hearing strange, unexplained sounds is one thing. Seeing a person who wasn't there was altogether a different matter. The woman's family was concerned for her well-being but was equally insistent that she was mistaken. Years later they discovered the woman had an intuitive capability that they didn't share. She had, in fact, heard babies crying, but they weren't alive. It was their spirit she had heard.

In 1957, three teenaged boys were milling about on the outskirts of St. John's when they came across a strangely shaped bundle. Curious as youth are, one of the boys kicked at the charred package that they thought, at the time, might have been the burned remains of a dog. To their horror, what they'd discovered was the corpse of not one, but two infants. The authorities were immediately called in and the discovery evolved into the province's most sensational unsolved murder case of the 1950s.

Dale Jarvis, author of *Haunted Shores*, described the first body as being "burned considerably, and covered with charred papers, tissue and bits of clothing." Judging by the decomposition of the second body, it was determined that infant had been deceased much longer, "though it was tidily dressed in a nightgown with handiwork around the throat. The second corpse was almost mummified, flattened to a thickness of about three inches, and dried and hard like a piece of board."

Anxious to get answers about what looked to be two murder cases, police went to the media. The headlines, and accompanying stories, caught the attention of a taxi driver who believed he knew something about the case. The man explained that he'd picked up a woman at 92 Queen's Road and driven her to the location where the bodies had been discovered. He testified that the woman had a package with her, and that she claimed it was filled with old clothes she wanted to get rid of. The cabbie must have wondered why she would have chosen to burn the box of clothes in a rural location instead of just throwing it in the trash. Nonetheless, he sat in his cab and waited for the woman to return.

After hearing the cabbie's story, police arrested a 37-year-old woman who, at the time, lived at 92 Queen's Road and charged her with the "illegal disposal of a human corpse." In court, the woman denied ever seeing the cab driver, much less having anything to do with the death and disposal of two babies. She also refused to explain why she had a large amount of cash on her when she was arrested. Was that money payment for what she'd allegedly done, the court wondered? If not, why did she refuse to explain how she'd earned it?

It seems the only evidence suggesting the woman was involved in the unfortunate demise and disposal of these two unnamed babies came from the cabbie. That resulted in a "his word against hers" scenario that couldn't stand up in a court of law, and the woman was found not guilty. As Jarvis reports, "It is written that she thanked her lawyer, tossed her hair back and smiled at the police officers as she left the room."

What, if anything, can be surmised by the cocky attitude of the defendant? Did the woman, in fact, get away with murder? Or was her crime that of accessory after the fact, and did someone else commit the dastardly deed? No doubt the family whose grandmother heard babies crying, and witnessed the form of a woman walking up the stairs, revisited their quick dismissal of her experience. Is it possible that had they engaged the elderly grandmother further on the matter, pushing her for details, they might have been able to provide police with clues that might have solved the mystery? Who was the woman walking up the stairs? And was she on a mission to end the earthly existence of two innocent babies?

Certainly not every resident of 92 Queen's Road has heard babies crying, or seen a woman's ghost wandering about. That said, there have been enough people with sensitivities to the paranormal that have come forward, sharing a similar experience. Perhaps the babies are still looking for justice.

Chapter 34

The Ghost of Holy Trinity

~

Any building can be creepy when you're alone and it's dark outside. Floors have a way of creaking for no apparent reason; the fast rush of air that occurs when the furnace kicks in disturbs the silence; the tap, tap, tap, of a tree branch knocks on a windowpane. The silence of the empty building echoes, making all these sounds, and so many others, that much more pronounced.

Rumours that a ghost lurks in the Holy Trinity Cathedral in Québec City are longstanding. Touted as the "first Anglican cathedral built outside the British Isles," the building was commissioned and paid for by King George III. Construction began on the Palladian-style structure on August 11, 1800. It took four years before the cathedral was ready to welcome worshippers. According to its website, "the Historic Sites and Monuments Board of Canada recognized the Cathedral of the Holy Trinity as a place of national historic significance for its historical and architectural values."

According to members of Québec's paranormal community, Holy Trinity is also recognized as one of the city's most haunted buildings and was featured on an episode of the television series *Creepy Canada*.

Initial reports that something was amiss in the building seem to have come from various organists over the years. It's not uncommon for an organist to practice for Sunday service when the church is empty, and the organists practicing at Holy Trinity began reporting the sounds of footsteps echoing throughout the building or doors slamming shut.

"I knew I was alone but would still get up, walk around and call out to see if someone had snuck into the church," one organist explained. "I always locked the entry doors as a precaution, but the interior doors opening and slamming shut were startling."

In the winter, this organist even admitted to checking for footsteps in the snow, yet he was never able to find anyone lurking about—at least, there was no physical being in the building with him. The organist tried to brush the experiences off as just his imagination running wild, and he practiced on. Still, time and time again he'd hear footsteps rushing up behind him only to turn and find himself alone. And he had the distinct feeling that he was being watched.

One day, this particular organist couldn't set aside his suspicions that there was a ghost in the building any longer. Once again he had that unnerving sensation of being watched, only this time when he looked up to the second floor balcony, "I saw what appeared to be the shadowy form of a woman moving between the pillars," he explained.

Other members of the church reported similar accounts. Another organist happened to be a dog lover and brought his dog with him wherever he could, including to the cathedral while he was practicing. A gentle creature, the man's dog had never so much as growled at a stranger and yet one night, for no apparent reason, the pet "rushed up and down the aisles snapping at the air."

At least one source reports that Queen Elizabeth II visited the cathedral in 1964. No one can argue that the Queen isn't the kind of person to succumb to wild imaginings. Yet like the organist above, the Queen glanced up into the balcony and saw what she believed was a ghostly figure hovering.

Exactly who the ghost could be is a question that has prompted several theories. In her account of the story, author Susan Smitten explains that because the paranormal activities were so widely reported, church officials engaged the talents of a medium to uncover an answer. After several visits, the medium believed he had a handle on the situation.

"He concluded that the ghostly activity resulted from a tragic murder that took place about 75 years after the cathedral was consecrated. The medium said he felt that a woman from a nearby religious order had become pregnant. After delivering the baby, she killed it to avoid persecution or rejection from the order and then buried the body under the floorboards near the organ. Beneath the organ, there is a crypt that contains the grave of one of the church's first bishops. Next to it is a smaller, unmarked grave. No church records exist to explain who is buried within, but the size indicates it is the grave of a small child."

Is it possible that the woman the medium believed murdered her newborn baby watches over its unmarked grave? Or is it simply that her spirit is doomed to roam this earth as punishment for her horrible crime?

The beautiful cathedral was one of eight stops during the 2002 ghost tour season, led by Laurie Thatcher. Aptly arranged, the tour took place at night, around the time the organists would have been practicing and noticed the ethereal presence. Thatcher noted several unexplained occurrences during her tours, from noticing cold spots in the building to the distinct feeling of "icy fingers" crawling "up her legs while she tried to tell a tour group the cathedral's story."

As with any other oral tradition, the story of paranormal phenomena in the Québec cathedral has morphed with many a telling. When researching the ghostly activities at Holy Trinity I came across several stories that mentioned a "resident narcoleptic woman" who was allegedly "buried alive near the church during an outbreak of cholera." Yet another scenario suggested a woman was actually entombed in the church's foundation during its construction, and it was her spirit that roamed the building.

Whatever the real story behind the haunting of Holy Trinity Cathedral Québec, one thing is certain: all visitors should make sure to say their prayers as they enter and again when they leave.

Chapter 35

Turmoil at Tod House

~

Unconventional. Peculiar. Some might have even used the term erratic when describing the late John Tod. A Scot by birth and an adventurer by nature, the man was as unique in his appearance as he was his behaviour. As American historian Hubert Howe Bancroft wrote, "Tod could no more tell his story seated in a chair than he could fly to Jupiter while chained to the Rock of Gibraltar; arms, legs and vertebrae were all brought into requisition, while high-hued information, bombed with oaths, burst from his breast like lava from Etna."

That said, the man certainly had a way with the ladies. He had no less than four wives; some sources suggest he may have had as many as seven. And from these unions he produced 10 offspring. Following his immigration to Canada, Tod worked as a trader for the Hudson's Bay Company, a career that took him across the country. When he retired, he settled in Victoria, near what is now the community of Oak Bay. In 1851, on 186 hectares (460 acres) of what is now prime real estate but was then a thickly forested landscape, Tod built a home designed to his unique specifications.

The house at 2564 Heron Street was formally recognized as a Canadian Historic Place on June 28, 1974. The building, described as a "rare and intact example of the French Canadian style, piece-sur-piece construction, which was used extensively by Hudson's Bay builders across Canada," still stands. Although it's considered to be the oldest house in Western Canada it is, as of the writing of this book, still an active residence.

As with anything that old, the boundary between rumour and fact is often blurred. Some sources have suggested that a series of tunnels was constructed that led from the house to the beach and was used to run contraband to boats in the Oak Bay harbour. Similar tunnels have been discovered in other locations, so there might have, at one time, been some merit to the stories.

Another suggestion that may have some merit is the widely held belief that Tod House is haunted.

Stories of the haunting gained momentum during the time Lieutenant Colonel Evans and his wife lived at the property. The couple purchased Tod House in 1944, and shortly before the deal was finalized Evans received a strange phone call. The caller refused to identify himself, but the person warned Evans that the property was haunted. Being reasonable, levelheaded sort of people, Evans and his wife didn't believe in ghosts.

It wasn't long before that belief was challenged.

The first public sign that something strange might be going on took place during a New Year's Eve party in the late 1940s. An old biscuit jar hanging on a hook in the kitchen started swinging and, despite their best efforts to stop it, continued to move for more than half an hour. The Colonel brushed it off, telling his guests that it was all in keeping with the character of the house. Other strange occurrences included windows that would open on their own, and a cellar door that would swing open even after a latch was installed to keep it closed.

Over time the couple began to notice the strange activity increased in winter, and in particular, during the Christmas season. One Yuletide morning they woke to find all their Christmas decorations had been removed from the tree and fireplace mantle and tossed on the floor.

There were also odd cold spots in the home, and a particularly eerie feeling in a large room that the couple had originally planned to use as their master bedroom. Needless to say, they opted to use another bedroom instead, and they used that room for guests. Two air force men stayed at the house for a weekend during World War II and spent a night in that room. According to an account documented in a BC Heritage website dedicated to the home, one guest awoke around midnight. He later told Ron Baird of the *News-Herald* a story that solidified the house's reputation for being haunted:

"We had been asleep for several hours when I suddenly awoke. I can't really describe what woke me, although it sounded like the rattling of chains. Over in the corner stood an Indian woman, her hands held out toward me in such a manner that she seemed to be pleading with me to help her. On her arms and legs were what looked like fetters. She kept looking at me, her hands outstretched and saying something that I couldn't catch. As suddenly as she appeared she was gone. I'll never forget the sight."

Following the experience, Colonel Evans researched the history of the house, and John Tod in particular, and discovered there were several stories about a First Nations woman floating about. Some suggested the man had hired such a woman as a housekeeper, and that she'd been so jealous when Tod returned from a trip to Scotland with a new wife that she went crazy and disappeared. Another version of the story suggests that Tod had actually married a dark-haired woman and that she'd gone insane. Tod's method of dealing with the situation was to chain her up in one of the rooms in his home—perhaps the very room the Colonel and Mrs. Evans originally wanted to use as their master bedroom.

Exactly who the spirit was and exactly what it wanted continued to be a mystery, but the reason why an ethereal being might refuse to leave the premises was unearthed in 1952. Evans and his wife decided to convert the home's heating system to oil, so workers needed to excavate a hole to house the storage tank. They'd dug about 2 metres before work had to cease—at least until the authorities arrived to collect the skeletal remains they had unearthed. Only bones remained, leaving investigators thinking that the body had been covered with copious amounts of lime to aide in its decomposition. After a thorough examination, it was determined the skeleton belonged to a woman who was possibly of First Nations or Asian descent. Was it possible that John Tod had indeed imprisoned one of his wives and, when she finally died, her tortured soul lingered on for all eternity?

It was widely believed that the paranormal activity at the Tod house ceased after the skeleton was exhumed and properly buried. Given the fact that there don't seem to be any reports of hauntings from residents who took over the property after the Evans family, the spirit may have very well entered into a peaceful rest.

Chapter 36

Honouring our Dead

~

Long before Europeans inhabited this country, First Nations peoples had raised families and lived off the land, roaming from one area to another depending on the season. This nomadic way of life was foreign to early settlers, but it worked well for generations of Natives.

A very small group of Inuit called the Netsilingmiut, or "people of the place where there is seal," lived on the Arctic coast, west of Hudson Bay. When Greenlandic explorer Knud Rasmussen visited the area in 1923, the Netsilingmiut numbered about 260 people. Amazingly, these people travelled the area between Committee Bay, Victoria Strait and Somerset Island, a territory of about 103,600 square kilometres.

These nomadic hunters travelled in small family packs, hunting seal and caribou or fishing for salmon and trout as they went. They used every part of each kill, making the bones into tools and skins into clothing. With the establishment of the Hudson's Bay Company post in the Boothia Peninsula in 1948, the Netsilingmiut were able to trade for knives, weapons and even wood with which they could build sleds and kayaks.

Even with the arrival of explorers and the subsequent formal communities with their schools and stores and Royal Canadian Mounted Police headquarters, the Netsilingmiut continued to maintain their traditional way of life. Birth and burial were just as ingrained in their way of living as were their hunting and fishing practices. So when an unnamed Netsiling-miut woman was murdered in the 1950s, custom dictated that her remains receive the dignity of a traditional send-off.

Unfortunately, the woman had been murdered some distance from her community of Taloyoak, which was then known as Spence Bay, and the settlers who found her did not know the Inuit customs. Because the ground was frozen, it was decided that her body would be brought to the Hudson's Bay Company post and stored in a cold room until the ground was thawed enough to bury her remains.

Perhaps the woman's spirit was disturbed by the fact that her earthly body had been placed in storage, like a seal carcass might have been. Or perhaps her ghost was calling out for justice, angry at her earthly life being cut short by a callous, unnamed murderer. Regardless the cause behind it, strange things began happening at the post.

Initially, those living at the post began noticing the sound of doors opening and closing at will, and footsteps rushing about when there was no one in sight. Then there was the sound of a woman whispering in the night, or making a coughing or gurgling sound as if gasping for air. Concerned, anyone who heard these sounds would rush out to investigate. As with the footsteps and the sound of doors closing, there was never anyone around who could have made the noise and yet, there was the very distinct feeling that someone, or something, was lurking nearby.

The strange occurrences were so frequent that people were becoming anxious. What was causing these sounds? Why was everyone feeling so on edge? They started backtracking in the attempt to determine when the sounds started and noticed that what seemed to be ghostly activity began when the murdered woman had been brought to the post. Was it possible the woman was calling out for help? Was she seeking justice? Or did she simply want to be laid to rest, adhering to her culture's traditions?

When the spring thaw finally arrived, the poor woman's body received a respectful but European burial. Reports of footsteps and a woman coughing ceased, leading most folks to believe her spirit had been appeased.

Chapter 37
Ghost Rider of Mount Hosmer

~

The small city of Fernie, BC, is a quaint and picturesque community nestled in the Elk Valley area of the East Kootenays. Often called the "Heart of the Rockies," it is acknowledged as the only city in Canada that is fully encircled by the Rocky Mountains; those mountains have not only provided the community with a thriving coal industry, they have also been the subject of a legend that dates back to the 1890s.

Fernie got its name from William Fernie, the 19th century prospector who is credited with having established the coal industry in the area. According to legend, that credit really belongs to a First Nations chief and his daughter. Having met the daughter during one of his expeditions, Fernie reportedly noticed an unusual necklace around the woman's neck. It was made of shiny black stones, and Fernie immediately recognized the stones as coal. He started quizzing the young woman about where they came from and quickly learned that the woman he'd

been flirting with was the chief's daughter. At that point he
decided to introduce himself to the leader of the tribe and question him directly about the black stones.

Most often people don't just fall into positions of leader-
ship, and the chief in this story was no exception. He was a wise
leader, and an even wiser father. He not only recognized what
Fernie was after, he was concerned for his daughter's welfare. He
decided that the best way to deal with Fernie was to become
partners. He'd provide the information on the location of the
coal and in turn, Fernie would become his son-in-law.

Although Fernie accepted the chief's proposal, he had no
intention of keeping his promise. As soon as Fernie knew the
location of the secret Morrissey Coal Seams he returned to his
own life, abandoning the young woman and her angry father. It
was a dishonourable, thankless move on Fernie's part, and the
chief would make sure the man, his ancestors and any others
who chose to move into the area and take advantage of the area's
resources would suffer. Some blame the chief, while other
sources hold the tribe's medicine woman responsible for the
tragedies that would strike the town of Fernie and the surrounding Elk Valley. A future marred by fire, floods and famine would
befall the white settlers to ensure they never forgot the wrong
committed by the man who they credited with establishing the
area's coal industry.

A review of the area's history certainly supports the legend that the angry chief made good on his threats. In 1904, the
same year the city was incorporated, a fire swept through the

community, causing a great deal of damage. Residents had barely recovered from that devastating experience when a wildfire whipped through the forest and into town four years later, this time destroying all but 23 buildings. After fighting through no less than five major fires over a six-year period, residents decided to attack their rebuilding project with new materials. Stone and brick structures were erected in the hope that any future fire would be more easily contained.

With the threat of fire addressed, residents breathed a sigh of relief. But that relief didn't last long, and in 1916 the Elk River overflowed, and flood waters threatened parts of the community.

Mining disasters were also far too common in the area. On May 22, 1902, the neighbouring town site of Coal Creek suffered one of the worst mining disasters in Canadian history. *The Cranbrook Herald* covered the disaster in depth, and an entire country mourned as they learned how 128 men lost their lives in an underground explosion in the No. 2 Mine. In 1917 another explosion, this time in the No. 3 Mine, cost 38 men their lives.

Along with these disasters that seemed to plague the unfortunate community, the Great Depression also had a profound effect on area residents. Looking back on a history of calamity and setbacks, residents began to ponder the legend of William Fernie and the curse his actions incurred. Could there be some truth behind it? Did Fernie's actions result in all those years of destruction, death and devastation?

Perhaps it was time to make things right with the long-deceased chief and his daughter.

The wheels were put into motion to call a truce between members of the Kootenay First Nations and area residents. On August 15, 1964, Ktunaxa Nation Chief Ambrose Gravell (Chief Red Eagle) invited Fernie Mayor James White to join him at a ceremonial assembly. Together the two leaders smoked the peace pipe, which symbolically signified a resolution between the two groups and finally lifted the curse.

Today, members of the Kootenay First Nations and non-aboriginal residents in the area live together in harmony. At the same time, it's always good to know one's history or perhaps bear the curse of repeating it. As a visual reminder of the original curse that once plagued the region, the "Ghost Rider of Mount Hosmer" appears on the rock face above the city on sunny, summer evenings. As the Fernie Chamber of Commerce once described it, "The 'ghost' is a spectacular shadow in the form of an Indian Princess sitting on a horse with her father, the chief, walking beside her, leading the horse."

While most residents feel confident that the curse has been lifted, it has been said that some First Nations people still refuse to camp overnight in the area unless there is no other alternative…just in case.

Chapter 38

La Salle's Cabin

~

The dictionary defines gold fever as the "greed and excitement caused by a gold rush." Greed is one of the seven deadly sins, and for good reason. Greed blinds us to what is good and honourable in favour of chasing some measure of wealth or power.

In 1896, gold was discovered in the Yukon, and by 1897 the Klondike Gold Rush was the talk of the country. The hopes of staking a claim and getting rich provoked a stampede of prospectors to the northernmost reaches of this country. In fact, the influx of people into the area ballooned the otherwise small population to such an extent that it became necessary to establish a police force to maintain law and order. This also led to the formation of the Yukon Territory in 1898.

Fred Nelson and his partner, Swanson, were among those early prospectors exploring the northern region in hopes of striking it rich. They'd been panning the mouth of O'Brien

Creek, near the confluence of the Yukon and Fortymile rivers, in an area that had drawn many prospectors before.

The pair was so intent on their mission that they neglected to shut down their expedition in time to make it back to Dawson before the winter set in full force. By the time they were heading back into town, the temperature had plummeted to a body-numbing −40°C. There was no way the men would survive the night out in the cold, even if they managed to erect a makeshift shelter and, by some miracle, start a fire.

Desperation was beginning to set in when they noticed a cabin in the distance. Obscured by the driving snow, it was difficult to determine exactly how far they were from the structure, but just seeing the dim image was enough to propel them onward.

"You sure that's not La Salle's old shack?" Swanson asked Nelson.

"It may well be, but the way I see it, we have no choice but to bed there for the night," Nelson said.

Swanson shook his head. Nelson, knowing what his partner was thinking, mulled over his own reservations about the situation.

A legend had circulated far and wide about the old prospector known only as La Salle. The man had lived in the area for most of his adult life, and when he built his cabin, he set down roots; he had no intention of moving on any time soon. No one dared to question the man about where he came from or if he had any family. He was far from an amiable sort of fellow and much preferred his own company to that of anyone else. For the most part, people kept their distance from the crotchety character.

Then one day in 1896, someone happened to call on the man and discovered his dead body on the floor of his small cabin. It was clear from the blood-soaked state of the body that the man had been murdered, but no suspect in the crime could be pinpointed. There was some speculation that Tanana peoples, who primarily lived in Eastern Alaska but were known to travel the area, were frustrated with the large influx of Europeans in the region and were responsible for the crime. Others whispered of a more greed-based reason, suggesting La Salle had found a large cache of gold and a fellow miner did him in and robbed him of his riches. Theories aside, La Salle's murderer was never brought to justice.

It had been several years since the prospector's body was found, but the story was as fresh as if it had occurred the week before. Nelson and Swanson might not have been long-time residents of the area, but they knew of the story. They also knew of the rumours surrounding La Salle's cabin.

La Salle was gone, but his cabin remained. It was one of a very few structures that could provide warmth and protection from the elements. In the years since the man's death, fur trappers and prospectors alike would sometimes use the cabin for shelter on bitter, winter nights. However, more often than not they just bypassed it altogether. Apparently La Salle was just as disposed toward company after his death as he had been during his life. Travellers passing by the structure reported hearing strange, eerie sounds that they believed came from inside the building. Those who were brave enough to walk to the door said they were suddenly overcome by feelings of dread or apprehension. The few that dared venture to open the door and go inside always found themselves racing to get away from some unseen force that they felt threatened their very existence.

Nelson and Swanson were both mulling over the stories of La Salle's angry and embittered spirit as they walked up to the cabin's front door. They both felt it, both acknowledged the unsettling feeling that a malevolent being occupied the small space behind that door. Looking to each other for support, the men took a minute to rally their courage. Swanson nodded to Nelson as the man reached for the door handle. The door swung open and both men entered.

It was hard to describe what they felt, though Nelson did his best when he shared his story with a reporter from the *Klondike Nugget*. Feelings aren't objective, they just are. And yet they can wield such a powerful force in one's life. Pushing aside their fear and the notion that La Salle's ghost might be outraged by their boldness at using his home, Swanson and Nelson set out to build a fire in the stove. The comforting warmth helped calm their unease, and before long both men fell asleep.

A few hours had passed when Nelson bolted upright. He heard a mournful sound in that haze between a deep sleep and being alert. At first he put it down to the wind whipping around the cabin, but now that he was fully awake he realized that the sound wasn't coming from outside the building. Rather, the moans sounded more like a man in distress, and they were coming from inside the cabin.

The noises had also aroused Swanson, and the men decided to see if someone had joined them for the night and was perhaps sleeping in the adjoining room. When they tried the door it wouldn't budge, which was strange because they'd checked out that room earlier and had no problem opening the door. Both men tried the handle, pushing the door with all their might. In the process Nelson believed he could hear a man's muffled pleas for help. Instructing Swanson to keep trying the door, Nelson threw on his parka and boots and rushed around the outside of the building to look through the window.

At this point neither Swanson nor Nelson were thinking a ghost was lurking in the building. Both men believed that someone had stumbled onto the cabin, just as they had, and not wanting to wake them, that person quietly made his way into the small room to rest where, for some reason, he found himself in a desperate state.

With his heart racing, Nelson brushed the snow off the windowpane and peered inside the room. He wasn't sure what he had expected to see, but he definitely wasn't prepared for what he saw. There, standing before him, was the transparent figure of a man, seemingly floating in the air. It looked like someone had sliced one side of the man's face open, and the large, bloody gash stretched from his temple to his throat. The ghost looked like he was pleading, begging for help, but the moans and groans only paralyzed Nelson with fear. Any drop of courage he had left pushed him to race back into the cabin to tell Swanson what he'd seen.

After hearing Nelson's story, Swanson had an idea. If the apparition in the other room was indeed a spirit reaching out for help, perhaps he should try to communicate with it. Swanson began by asking the spirit if it was La Salle's ghost. In response to the question, the phantom knocked on the door. Swanson asked if the ghost knew the person who killed him and, in response, the knocks got louder. When Swanson asked if the ghost could identify his killer, the door burst open. Standing before Nelson and Swanson was the ghost of La Salle with his arms reaching out towards them and a light emanating from its form. Shocked by the ghost's sudden aggressive behaviour, the men screamed, and the image vanished before their eyes.

Deciding they'd seen enough, and not wanting to provoke the spirit any further, Nelson and Swanson hastily packed up their supplies and left the cabin. They could see the smoke billowing from the chimney, fading into the night sky just as the ghost had vanished before them.

It's not known if the pair of prospectors ever returned to the area or just gave up on a prospecting career altogether. Nelson was so visibly terrified by the experience that anyone listening to the tale never questioned that Nelson and his partner had indeed come face to face with La Salle's ghost. Unfortunately, references to this story are rare indeed, and it's unknown if the murdered man's spirit ever entered into its eternal rest, or if it is still calling out for help.

Chapter 39

Going Wendigo

~

The preceding stories have all suggested that a ghost or unsettled spirit was the result of a violent life, or a violent demise. But there have been cases in history where an evil spirit has been said to possess an individual, pushing them to do terrible things.

This is the story of Ka-Ki-Si-Sutchin. Known also as Swift Runner, the 6-foot, 3-inch Cree hunter made a good living for himself and his family. He'd worked as a guide for the North-West Mounted Police (NWMP) from the time the force arrived in central Alberta in 1873 until that winter of 1878. The weather was bitterly cold that year, and even a seasoned and capable hunter like Swift Runner had trouble putting dinner on the table. He was also cold and living in a makeshift hut.

Truth be told, Swift Runner came into quite the unfavourable predicament that winter. Previously, he and his wife, six children, his mother and brother all resided with his tribe, but things had changed. The amiable, well-respected hunter had fallen into disrepute after he'd developed a love for the taste of whisky. It wasn't the drinking that was the problem; it was the fact that he turned into a feral monster when he drank. Nobody could control him and as a result, the members of his tribe didn't want him around when he was under the influence. Swift Runner had brought shame to his people, and he and his family were banished to the backcountry.

In any other year the banishment from his tribe may not have been so difficult. Swift Runner was at home in the wilderness. He found peace there. And yet that year he'd been plagued with a melancholy so profound he just couldn't shake it off. Surely the inclement weather was making the situation worse, Swift Runner reasoned with himself. It certainly didn't help that his wife and family were struggling and obviously unhappy because of him. The old adage was true even then: happy wife, happy life.

The voices didn't help matters any. They were whispers, really, coming from the woods. It was as if they were beckoning him, but not in the peaceful way they had in the past. These whispers made him feel anxious and agitated, and that creature lurking about didn't help. Nobody else had noticed it; nobody else had Swift Runner's keen senses. The creature was calling to him; it was everywhere he looked. It was even invading his dreams. And it was telling him to do something terrible, something that didn't make sense even with a bottle's worth of whisky in his belly. The problem was the voices wouldn't stop until he followed through with their request, Swift Runner was certain.

Then he would be left alone. There would be no family to watch out for, and no voices to continue prodding him.

No one knew of Swift Runner's plight until the following spring when he arrived at the Catholic Mission in St. Albert. When people asked where his family was, they weren't prepared for his reply. They were all dead, he said. When questioned further he explained the family died of starvation, and his wife had committed suicide.

Swift Runner's explanation didn't ring true to anyone at the mission. The family was all in good health when they'd last come through the previous winter, and the 200-pound man standing before them didn't look like he'd gone without food. Also, there was something disturbing about the man's demeanour. His eyes had a vacant look to them, and yet for someone who'd lost his entire family, he didn't look to be grieving. The priests at the mission shared their concerns with the NWMP who, in turn, approached Swift Runner. A trip to the man's campsite was organized.

They certainly weren't prepared for what their search would unearth.

There was indeed a grave, and it held the body of one of Swift Runner's young sons. Without the benefit of a coroner at the site to investigate, it seemed the boy may have died from natural causes.

The human bones littering the campsite, on the other hand, were an altogether different matter.

Inspector Severe Gagnon was one of the officers accompanying Swift Runner that day. When he asked the trapper about the moccasin-stuffed human skull he'd just picked up, Gagnon was startled by the man's honest reply.

"That was my wife," he simply said. The smaller bones belonged to his children, the others to his brother and mother. Aside from the bones, so bare even the marrow was gone, there were no other signs of Swift Runner's family.

Gagnon pressed Swift Runner for an explanation, and a story about starvation and suicide wouldn't do. So Swift Runner told the officer the truth.

The spirit of Wendigo had taken over Swift Runner's body. The hunter tried to ignore its demand for human flesh but he was finally overcome. Wendigo had forced Swift Runner to kill and consume every member of his family, with the exception of the son who had died before the carnage began.

Author Bruce Wishart explained that Swift Runner told the officers present that Wendigo had forced one of Swift Runner's boys to "kill and butcher his younger brother" and then the spirit had forced Swift Runner to hang his "infant by the neck from a lodge pole and [tug] at the baby's dangling feet."

It was a story so bizarre that it had to be true. It was a horrific scene, and a horrific story. Officers arrested Swift Runner, charging him with the murder of at least eight of his family members. They collected whatever human remains hadn't been carried off by scavenging animals and travelled with Swift Runner to Fort Saskatchewan.

In his book, *The Manitous: The Spiritual World of the Ojibway*, scholar Basil Johnston writes that of all "the evil beings who dwelt on the periphery of the world of the Anishinaubae peoples, none was more terrifying than the Wendigo. It was a creature loathsome to behold and as loathsome in its habits, conduct and manners." Many First Nations legends throughout the northern U.S. and parts of Canada describe the spirit of Wendigo as a cannibalistic demon that is never satisfied with anything but human flesh. He is a large beast that grows with every killing, and the larger he grows the hungrier he becomes. He is the personification of greed and excess. It is also believed that the spirit could possess people, who in turn, would embody its characteristics.

By his own admission, Swift Runner had "gone Wendigo," which pushed him to kill and consume the members of his family. "Wendigo psychosis" is the actual clinical term for someone possessing a seemingly unquenchable desire for human flesh. Despite the fact that the fear of being attacked by the spirit was very much a part of the culture in northern Alberta's aboriginal communities in the late 19th century, the legitimacy of this disorder is still a matter of debate. Posing this as a defence back in 1879 would not have swayed a jury to leniency. So despite his obvious remorse at what he had done, and his insistence that Wendigo had taken over his body and mind and he was a mere vehicle in the murders, Swift Runner admitted to the crimes. "The least of men," he reportedly called himself. "[I] do not merit even being called a man." He was ashamed that he, the mighty hunter, wasn't strong enough to fend off the monster in his mind.

Swift Runner went to trial on August 8, 1879. Although the Cree and Métis jurors knew of the Wendigo legends and understood their power, they found Swift Runner guilty. He was hanged on December 20, 1879, making Swift Runner the first legal hanging in what is now Alberta.

Swift Runner's encounter with the Wendigo was the most devastating in our country's history, but it certainly wasn't the only cannibalistic murder attributed to possession by an evil spirit. Thankfully, others claiming to be under the evil spirit's influence were stopped before their crimes escalated to the number of deaths in Swift Runner's case.

Is it possible that the spirit of a monster can seize control of a person's mind and body and cause them to commit such abhorrent acts of violence? Admittedly, stories of such demon possession aren't as common as they might have been in the past, but that doesn't mean it hasn't happened.

Notes on Sources

Asfar, Dan. *Haunted Highways.* Edmonton: Lone Pine Publishing, 2003

Belanger, Jeff. *The World's Most Haunted Places.* Wayne: New Page Books, 2004.

Belyk, Robert C. *Spirits of the West: Eerie Encounters from the Prairies to the Pacific.* Victoria: TouchWood Editions, 2014.

——— *Ghosts: True Tales of Eerie Encounters.* Victoria: TouchWood Editions, 2002.

Butts, Edward. *Ghost Stories of Newfoundland and Labrador.* Toronto: Dundurn Press, 2010.

Christensen, Jo-Anne. *Ghost Stories of British Columbia.* Toronto: Dundurn Press, 1996.

Da Silva, Maria and Andrew Hind. *More Ontario Ghost Stories.* Edmonton: Lone Pine Publishing, 2012.

Hancock, Pat. *Haunted Canada 3: More True Ghost Stories.* Toronto: Scholastic Canada Ltd., 2007.

Houghton, Margaret. *The Hamiltonians: 100 Fascinating Lives.* Toronto: James Lorimer & Company Ltd., 2003.

Jarvis, Dale. *Haunted Shores: True Ghost Stories of Newfoundland and Labrador.* St. John's: Flanker Press, 2004.

Johnston, Basil. *The Manitous: The Spiritual World of the Ojibway.* St. Paul: Minnesota Historical Society Press, 1995.

Marlowe, John. *Canadian Mysteries of the Unexplained: Investigations into the Fantastic, the Bizarre and the Disturbing.* London: Arcturus Publishing, 2009.

Melady, John. *Double Trap: The Last Public Hanging in Canada.* Toronto: Dundurn Press, 2005.

Oickle, Vernon. *Ghost Stories of Nova Scotia.* Lunenburg: MacIntyre Purcell Publishing Inc., 2015.

——— *Ghost Stories of the Maritimes: Volume II.* Edmonton: Lone Pine Publishing, 2002.

Schneck, Robert Damon. "Ghostbuster: Charles Edgar DeWolfe was so sure that Windsor, Nova Scotia, was haunted that he invited a New York psychic researcher (Hereward Carrington) to investigate..." *The Beaver* 82, 5 (Oct.-Nov. 2002): 23-7.

Shaw, Rob. "Cold Case: Donna Mitchell: Leads in slaying went cold with suspect's suicide." *The Victoria Times Colonist,* 27 September 2008.

Skelton, Robin. *A Gathering of Ghosts: Haunting and Exorcisms from the Personal Casebook of Robin Skelton and Jean Kozocari.* Vancouver: Douglas & McIntyre, 1989.

Smith, Barbara. *Deadly Encounters: True Crime Stories of Alberta.* Toronto: Dundurn Press, 1994.

——— *Ghost Stories and Mysterious Creatures of British Columbia.* Edmonton: Lone Pine Publishing, 1999.

——— *Haunted Alberta: 62 True Ghost Stories.* Edmonton: Lone Pine Publishing, 2009.

——— *More Ghost Stories of Alberta.* Edmonton: Lone Pine Publishing, 1996.

Smitten, Susan, et. al. *Canadian Ghost Stories: Volume II.* Edmonton: Lone Pine Publishing, 2003.

Underhill, Doug. *Miramichi: Tales Tall & True.* Saint John: Neptune Publishing Company, Ltd., 1999.

Web Sources

www.barkerville.com/vol2/blssing1.htm

www.barkerville.com/vol2/blssing2.htm

bcgoldrushpress.com/2012/10/murder-charles-blessing

hubpages.com/religion-philosophy/The-Doppleganger-of-Beacon-Hill-Park-The-story-behind-the-haunting-Part-1

www.canada.com/travel/ghost+hunting+alberta+badlands/5598415/story.html

bouncingpinkball.wordpress.com/2009/10/30/the-keenan-bridge-ghost/

cbc.ca/news/canada/covered-bridge-destroyed-by-fire-1.286352

executedtoday.com/2011/12/07/1869-nicholas-melady-the-last-public-hanging-in-canada/

www.hauntednorthamerica.org/hauntedlocation.aspx?id=658 huron county goal ghosts

www.archive.org/stream/historyofcourtof00townuoft#page/n5/mode/2up

montrealmosaic.com/attraction/griffintown-and-point-st-charles-heritage-trail

ocprstoronto.wordpress.com/2012/09/04/the-ghost-of-mary-gallagher-27th-june-2012/

www.angelsghosts.com/fort_saskatchewan_museum_ghost_stories

www.canada.com/edmonton/edmontonjournal/soundoff/story.html?id=35518c21-2099-4989-890e-aec7ff1c0181

www.fortsaskatchewanrecord.com/2014/11/06/notorious-hangings-in-the-fort

www.executedtoday.com/2014/05/02/1923-florence-lassandro-unwilling-feminist/

www.thespec.com/news-story/2268914-a-crime-so-brazen-violent-and-senseless-/

1876inhamilton.blogspot.ca/2012/01/january-24-1876.html

news.ourontario.ca/newmarket/114651/page/3

www.taxi-library.org/canada/1-b12.htm

www.virtualmuseum.ca/sgc-cms/histoires_de_chez_nous-community_
memories/pm_v2.php?id=story_line_child&fl=&lg=English&ex=00000599&sl
=4842&pos=14&scpos=1 newspaper account double hanging

www.prairieghosts.com/ambrose.html

www.mysteriesofcanada.com/alberta/lost-lemon-mine/

news.google.com/newspapers?nid=37&dat=19060209&id=mIwmAAAAIBAJ&
sjid=5TUDAAAAIBAJ&pg=2809,3233958&hl=en

ocprstoronto.wordpress.com/2011/07/27/gibraltar-point-lighthouse—-the-
legend-exposed/

torontoist.com/2009/10/toronto_haunts/

www.fortyork.ca/images/newsletters/fife-and-drum-2015/fife-and-drum-
dec-2015.pdf Radan Mueller

spacing.ca/toronto/2015/04/30/true-story-torontos-island-ghost/

www.dailymail.co.uk/femail/article-2251233/1950s-voted-desirable-era-
modern-women-desperate-men-make-effort.html

www.canada.com/story.html?id=b7fa82a9-2a08-4746-8015-e34a5ed27267

www.aubergewillow.com/en/about-us/

www.hauntedplaces.org/item/auberge-willow-place-inn/

www.historicplaces.ca/en/rep-reg/place-lieu.aspx?id=6841

www.ghostsofvancouver.com/century_house.htm

www.archivesalberta.org/odd/mummy.htm

www.mysteriesofcanada.com/new-brunswick/dungarvon-whooper/

www.memoriesofblackville.com/history/legend-of-the-dungarvon-whooper/

www.geist.com/fact/essays/the-ghost-of-james-cawdor/

www.ghosttowns.com/canada/ontario/silverislet.html

ontarioplaques.com/Plaques/Plaque_ThunderBay18.html

www.thetelegram.com/Opinion/Columnists/2014-12-15/article-3976088/
Smoker,-the-ghostly-trapper-of-Labrador/1

lanesprivateerinn.wordpress.com

www.travellingrubberchicken.com/2010/06/ghostly-woman-in-Québec-city.html

basementgeographer.com/tragedies-of-the-crowsnest-pass-part-ii/

tourismfernie.com/history/legends-myths

www.edmontonjournal.com/news/hanged/index.html

www.brucewishart.com/solidgold/windigo

hauntedsitesincanada.weebly.com